Country Roads of
NEW JERSEY

Drives, Day Trips, and Weekend Excursions

Third Edition

Judi Dash and Jill Schensul

COUNTRY ROADS PRESS
NTC/Contemporary Publishing Group

Library of Congress Cataloging-in-Publication Data

Dash, Judi.
    Country roads of New Jersey : drives, day trips, and weekend excursions /
Judi Dash and Jill Schensul.—3rd ed.
       p.   cm.—(Country roads)
    Includes index.
    ISBN 1-56626-022-1
    1. New Jersey—Tours.   2. Automobile travel—New Jersey—Guidebooks.
3. Rural roads—New Jersey—Guidebooks.   I. Schensul, Jill.   II. Title.
III. Series.
F132.3.D37   1999
917.4904'43—dc21   98-46389
                                                      CIP

Cover and interior design by Nick Panos
Cover illustration copyright © Todd L. W. Doney
Interior site illustrations and map copyright © Leslie Faust
Interior spot illustrations copyright © Barbara Kelley
Picture research by Elizabeth Broadrup Lieberman

Published by Country Roads Press
A division of NTC/Contemporary Publishing Group, Inc.
4255 West Touhy Avenue, Lincolnwood (Chicago), Illinois 60646-1975 U.S.A.
Copyright © 1994, 1996, 1999 by Judi Dash and Jill Schensul
Printed in the United States of America
International Standard Book Number: 1-56626-022-1

99 00 01 02 03 ML 18 17 16 15 14 13 12 11 10 9 8 7 6 5 4 3 2 1

To David and Paul

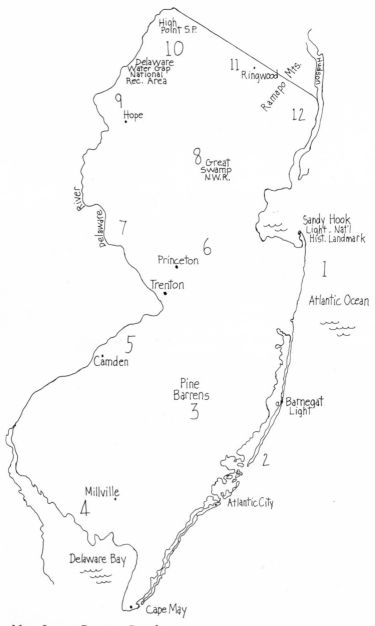

New Jersey Country Roads
(Figures correspond with chapter numbers.)

Contents

Acknowledgments

Judi and Jill would like to lovingly thank their respective mates, David Molyneaux and Paul Wilder, for their patience and support during the research and writing of this book, and for their often invaluable help in navigating the country roads of New Jersey. Jill would also like to thank her dog, Poncho, although he was no help at all.

Introduction

"I don't like the beach; I don't like nature; I like New Jersey."

—A character in the off-Broadway play
Lips Together, Teeth Apart.

Clearly, if that character ever visited the Garden State, she never ventured off the New Jersey Turnpike. The state is 24 percent farmland and has a million acres of pine forest, 1,400 miles of prime trout streams, 800 lakes and ponds, and 127 miles of Atlantic coastline, much of it pristine beaches.

Hikers trek the Appalachian Trail in the state's wild northwest, fishing enthusiasts trawl for record-breakers in the deep south's Delaware Bay, antique lovers scout for bargains in the rural communities of Lambertville, Andover, Lafayette, and Mullica Hill, and naturalists canoe through the mysterious Pine Barrens—at 1.1 million acres it's the largest wilderness area east of the Mississippi. And back east, folks can board the ferry to Ellis Island and the Statue of Liberty from Jersey City's Liberty State Park, stroll the miles and miles of boardwalk in communities all along the Atlantic shoreline, or track migrating birds and whales off the coast of Cape May.

There's history everywhere: at battlefields where cannons sit a lonely vigil and monuments pay tribute to fallen patriots; at re-created Colonial villages with lively demonstrations of early American crafts; at museums that trace the state's industrial evolution in mining, glassmaking, shipping, and manufacturing; in the venerable halls and haunts of mighty learning institutions like Princeton University; and at old houses in proud towns where a plaque on the door or a little sign in the yard bears testament to settlers, seafarers, and movers and shakers through the years.

A driving trip is as much about getting out of the car and into the heart of country life as it is about moving on down the road. We'll tell you where to explore on foot in both pastoral and populated locales. You can take long strolls along old canals, around quiet lakes and sleepy towns, and through myriad parklands with ecosystems ranging from salt marsh to pine forest to sandy expanses of dunes. Or you can join in the life of a community at country fairs and bustling cafés, and even (this will be our secret) shopping outlets.

We'll also tell you about great places to bike and canoe, or to just settle back and let someone else do the navigating—on a trolley tour, a whale-watching expedition, a glider ride.

Of course, you've got to eat, and we'll take you to candle-lit inns, bounteous farm stands, and great places to savor the freshest seafood. When it's time to bed down, you may opt for an aged stone-walled inn, delicate Victorian gingerbread bed and breakfasts, or just a simple cheap sleep close to the action. We wish that all the routes in this book were picturesque, but, progress being what it is, there are times when you'll have to travel for short distances along roads lined with strip malls and other eyesores. Never fear. We'll get you back to the good stuff as soon as possible—and for as long as possible.

The New Jersey Division of Travel and Tourism publishes a helpful travel guide to the state, which summarizes the high points of each region and lists hotels, restaurants, parks, campgrounds, and other points of interest. The state also publishes three specialty guides: *The New Jersey Outdoor Guide, The New Jersey Cultural and Historic Guide,* and the *New Jersey Calendar of Events.* For free copies of the guides, call the tourism office's toll-free number: 800-JERSEY-7.

You'll need a good map for these trips. We've tried to give you very specific and up-to-date directions, but community development and a seemingly statewide penchant for changing route numbers can wreak havoc on even the most carefully researched road data. Don't hesitate to ask directions when in doubt.

When we set out to write this book, we worried that we wouldn't find enough "country" in New Jersey to fill 12 chapters. We ended up so overloaded with gorgeous rural towns, roads, and byways that we had to prune our selections, leaving out some great places. You'll just have to ferret them out for yourself!

New Jersey is truly a state filled with grace and beauty, and you've only to get off the highway to discover it. When you do, you're in for a wonderful surprise.

1

North Shore Ramble

Getting there: Take the Garden State Parkway to exit 82, then State 37 east across Barnegat Bay to the Barnegat Peninsula, and follow the signs south to Island Beach State Park, where our trip begins. If you're a bicycling enthusiast, by all means bring your bike, park the car along the roadside once you reach Seaside Park, just north of Island Beach, and cycle the 10-mile-long narrow road through the state park.

Highlights: Long stretches of deserted dunes, salt marshes with spectacular bird-watching, quiet seaside towns, bicycling and boardwalk strolls, and majestic lighthouses.

This weekend journey takes us along some of the prettiest parts of the state's North Shore, from the Barnegat Peninsula's beautiful Island Beach State Park northward to the gracious resort communities of Mantoloking, Manasquan, Sea Girt, Spring Lake, Avon-by-the-Sea, and Ocean Grove, and the historic lighthouses of Sandy Hook and Highlands.

Cattus Island County Park Detour

A short detour off State 37 en route to the Barnegat Peninsula is a must for nature lovers. Turn north on County Spur 549 (Fischer Boulevard) at its intersection with State 37 in Dover Township; watch for the park sign on your right about 1.5 miles up the road. A 500-acre expanse with salt marshes (great for bird-watching), pine and oak forests, cedar swamps, and some 300 species of plants and flowers, Cattus Island is actually a peninsula that looks like an island when the surrounding marshes are inundated by the tides. There are six miles of marked trails, a four-mile-long fire road, and an extensive boardwalk that provides park accessibility for wheelchairs and fun for all. The Cooper Environmental Center on the grounds has slide shows on the area's history; during the Revolutionary War, locals used to bring captured British vessels into nearby Toms River to off-load their cargo. An animal and dinosaur "tracking garden" was established in 1995; the garden is a place for kids and parents to learn about and make casts of prints left by wildlife. The center offers tours of the park and environs on weekends, and has numerous environmental programs for kids. In the summer you can take boat trips with a naturalist to explore surrounding sea life.

After visiting Cattus Island, return south on County 549 to State 37 east, crossing the causeway to the Barnegat Peninsula and Island Beach State Park.

With 3,000 acres of ocean beach, sculptured sand dunes, and saltwater marshes, Island Beach State Park is one of the last relatively undisturbed stretches of barrier island in the state. Many New Jerseyans don't know about this gorgeous expanse of usually uncrowded white sand with its great sea views. You could spend an entire day exploring the park, so allow at least a few hours to savor its splendors. (Warning: at the height of the summer season, park officials close the park to cars after the lots fill up, so, in good weather, get there early.)

About a mile south of the park entrance, be sure to stop at the Island Beach Aeolium, a welcome center where a park officer will be happy to orient you to the unique and fragile ecosystem of the area and to suggest the best wildlife viewing spots. This little nature center also has a wide range of pamphlets on bird and plant life, and there's a listing of daily nature walks, birding treks, children's activities, and seining excursions, in which you walk slowly through the water dragging a little net to gather marine life. From the Aeolium, a short self-guided nature walk makes a loop through a plant identification trail with 25 numbered stops.

During the late spring and summer, the mosquitoes here can be ravenous—very hot and overcast days are the worst—so bring along repellent, and check with park officials about the advisability of tackling the marsh.

The road heading south through the park is flanked by low pines and scrub bushes, punctuated with undulating dunes that grow progressively higher the farther south you go. Periodically, narrow cuts through the dune lands indicate beach access for pedestrians and all-terrain vehicles, the latter marring the pristine look of the place. There's no parking along the roadside; you must keep going until you encounter one of the lots spaced throughout the park.

At the end of the road, parking lot number 23 provides access to the park's most beautiful stretch of beach. A 1.5-mile walk takes you to the southern tip of the peninsula, where you'll get a great view across a narrow bridge to the Barnegat Lighthouse, affectionately known as Old Barney, which presides over the northern tip of Long Beach Island. The walk is a delightful one—we like to take along a picnic lunch and eat overlooking the lighthouse. The ocean here has a strong salty smell and you can watch waves crashing against the shore, fishermen standing knee-deep in water casting their lines, and, farther out, pleasure boats zooming to and fro. Because this beach is the farthest from the park entrance and there are a limited number of parking places, it is seldom crowded. There are no concession stands or rest rooms down here, but then that's part of the wild charm of the place.

Returning north toward the park entrance, pull into parking lot A20 and walk about 100 feet south down the road to the Spizzle Creek Bird Observation Blind. The approach trail through a marshy area (slather on insect repellent in summer) takes you to a small wooden building, screened on three sides, that overlooks the Sedge Islands—marshy land masses floating in Barnegat Bay. The islands are home to the largest concentrated osprey colony in New Jersey, with 18 nesting pairs atop towering platforms. A good set of binoculars will give you a great view of the birds; if you're lucky, you may also see peregrine falcons, herons, and egrets winging over the marsh.

Leaving Island Beach State Park the way you entered, drive north through the Barnegat Peninsula; the road takes in the best and worst of the barrier island. The ocean beaches and bayside harbors are uniformly lovely (in summer you'll need to purchase beach badges to take advantage of the former), but the towns themselves range from quiet havens amid the dunes where you'll want to stroll for hours, to loud amusement arcades you may want to get through as soon as possible. In the southern portion of the peninsula, Seaside Park, abutting Island Beach State Park, is the most idyllic of the towns. In the north, Normandy Beach and Mantoloking are knock-'em-dead gorgeous, with extensive dunes and stately beachfront mansions. Here the Barnegat Peninsula is at its narrowest, and at some points you have only to turn your head to see the ocean on one side and the bay on the other. The main road through the Barnegat Peninsula is State 35 (southbound views are mainly of Barnegat Bay, northbound of the Atlantic

Ocean), but be sure to get off on side streets whenever possible for a more intimate look at the resort communities and the kinds of architecture inspired by the two bodies of water.

At the north end of the peninsula, Bay Head is a lively community with several hotels and bed and breakfasts. A great place to stop for picnic food is Central Market on State 35, toward Point Pleasant. There's a good selection of wines and cheeses, and the staff is very friendly.

North of Bay Head, Point Pleasant Beach, the northernmost and largest town on the Barnegat Peninsula, calls itself the Seafood Capital of New Jersey. Point Pleasant is home to one of the four commercial fishing fleets in the state, and its restaurants (the best are on Channel Drive and Inlet Drive) are always stocked with fresh seafood.

State 35 north takes you over the broad Manasquan River. To your right the view is of salty marshland; on the left the river widens into a world of fishing, pleasure boats, and public beaches. The view is extra dramatic when the drawbridge is up and the larger boats sail through, perhaps bound for the Intracoastal Waterway, which stretches all the way to Florida. A boater entering the Manasquan Inlet here can cruise the entire passage without ever having to venture into the Atlantic Ocean.

Once over the river, you'll be in the upscale community of Brielle, an immaculate little town with lots of Victorian houses on the edge of the Manasquan River. The town is headquarters for a large fleet of charter and party boats. Especially popular are the *River Queen* and *River Belle*, Mississippi-style riverboats berthed at the Brielle Basin (signs throughout town direct you there; the boats cruise the Manasquan River with cocktails and dinner on board). Nearby, the Brielle Yacht Club

Restaurant is open to the public and is a great place to enjoy a drink overlooking the river action.

After Brielle, take the right fork off State 35 onto State 71 north, which continues up the coast through the communities of Manasquan, Sea Girt, Spring Lake, and Ocean Grove— some of the North Shore's prime beach communities with sizable year-round populations.

Each community along State 71 (also known as Ocean Avenue in most towns) has its own special charm: Manasquan, with its Victorian houses and heavily shaded streets, retains a nautical flavor from its seafaring days; Sea Girt has lots of pretty bays and inlets as well as a restored lighthouse at Ocean and Beacon Avenues dating from 1896.

Our hands-down favorite town on the North Shore is Spring Lake, just north of Sea Girt. Allow extra time to explore the community (spend the night if possible), which has a sprawling lake with willow-shaded benches and wooden bridges, meticulously manicured emerald green lawns, gingerbread cottages, and a two-mile-long boardwalk patrolled in season by bicycle-riding cops wearing shorts and sneakers.

Spring Lake is as popular for what it lacks as for what it has—it's kind of Cape May without the mini-malls and with a fraction of the crowds. Rigorous zoning has ensured that no arcades or concession stands abut the quiet boardwalk, no T-shirt shops or fast-food places mar the pretty cross streets. In fact all commercial establishments are confined to the small business district on and around Third Avenue, set many streets back from the beach and prime residential zone. Even the business district retains a certain classiness, with sloping awnings, pastel shingles, and dainty shop signs.

In summer there are outdoor concerts at the gazebo in Potters Park at Fifth and Warren Avenues, and theater groups perform year-round. Each June there's a historic house tour, and in early December the annual Victorian Christmas weekend offers visitors a chance to tour some of the town's most beautiful bed and breakfasts all decked out in seasonal decor.

Spring Lake is a great base for exploring the North Shore. Our favorite of the town's numerous bed and breakfasts is Sea Crest by the Sea, on Tuttle Avenue just a block from the ocean. If you'd rather stay at a bona fide hotel, the Breakers, right across from the ocean at Newark Avenue, is a good bet, as is the venerable Warren Hotel on Mercer Avenue.

A great way to get oriented is with a ride on the Spring Lake Trolley, which is actually a bus made to look like a trolley. It costs only $1, and passengers can hop on and off anywhere along the 6.5-mile route, which takes in most of the town's prime spots. No point in town is more than two blocks from a trolley stop. The trolley runs throughout the summer daily from 10:00 A.M. to 5:00 P.M.

Once you've gotten a sense of the town from the trolley ride, take to the streets on foot or bike. Among the prettiest roads with some of the finest 19th-century buildings are Tuttle, Jersey, Mercer, Sussex, Monmouth, Atlantic, and Union. The Chamber of Commerce distributes free walking and biking guides to Spring Lake, and if you're staying over, many of the bed and breakfasts provide bikes for guest use. The closest bike rental is about a five-minute drive north—in Belmar at D.J.'s Bicycle Shop, Fifteenth and Main Streets.

When we visit Spring Lake, we always head to the boardwalk at dusk. A long stroll gazing out on the breakers, with sea gulls diving for fish, puts us in the mellowest of moods and is a great way to greet the quiet night.

Though the town is certainly no shopping mecca, a few stores stand out as musts: the Third Avenue Chocolate Shoppe has sinful chocolate truffles; Vitales on Morris Street off Third has all kinds of marvelous clocks, some costing as much as $40,000; and Marcel Darché's Butcher Block at 1210 Third Avenue is a gourmet food store that's a great place to get picnic provisions.

Allaire State Park Detour

Just a 20-minute drive from Spring Lake (head west on Ludlow Street, which becomes County 524, and look for the signs) is one of New Jersey's prettiest parks. Allaire State Park has easy hiking trails through pine stands, bogs, and blueberry patches. The park is home to lovely Allaire Village, a restored 1800s town from the boom days of the bog-iron industry. Old-timey craft demonstrations are presented throughout the summer; and the Pine Creek Railroad, an authentic steam locomotive with a big red caboose, makes short runs around the park with much clanging and horn-tooting to please the kiddie set.

Stop first at the large visitors center, which has displays about the region's history, and pick up a self-guided walking tour pamphlet.

Walking through Allaire Village, past its ironworks, blacksmith shop, and bakery, try to imagine an 1830s community of 400 people who prospered turning the indigenous bog iron into pots and kettles that were in demand far and wide.

Sadly, the town declined in the 1850s because of competition from higher grade iron ore being mined in Pittsburgh. What you'll see are the restored remains of the once wealthy community—some 20 buildings set against a background of woods and meadows, with little wooden bridges crossing skinny creeks. Park employees in period dress will tell you about how buildings were used and what life was like for the inhabitants.

Heading north from Spring Lake via Ocean Boulevard, you'll pass through a large, ornate gate (which in the old days actually closed to keep out undesirables) into Belmar. But you don't need the gate to know you're changing towns. Belmar is to Spring Lake what Motel 6 is to The Ritz. This is real *Beach*

Blanket Bingo territory—with lots of pizza places and tourist shops marring the oceanfront.

Keep on going north through the pretty seaside towns of Avon-by-the-Sea and Bradley Beach to Ocean Grove, a town with a fascinating history that still permeates the mood and daily life of the place.

Founded in 1869 as a Methodist summer campground, the town is still a religious retreat. Among other things, you can't get liquor in town—or get onto the beach before 12:30 P.M. on Sunday. In the old days, on Sunday the town leaders closed up the whole community, chaining the gates so no one could get in or out. If you were here, you went to church—or else.

Come summer, families occupy tents that flank the community's imposing orange Great Auditorium, found at the western end of Ocean Pathway. The auditorium is used for church services, Bible study, and organ concerts, as well as performances by big-name entertainers who are deemed wholesome enough for family viewing.

Especially interesting are the 114 tents alongside the Great Auditorium. Part canvas and part wooden bungalow, with open porches and flower gardens, many of these dwellings have been rented summer after summer by generations of the same family, who come to Ocean Grove to pray, attend camp meetings, and sunbathe in the company of people who share their religious and moral ideals. Stop and chat with one of the residents and you'll likely be invited into his or her tent for a tour and a cup of coffee.

Start your Ocean Grove exploration at the Visitors Bureau at 64 Main Avenue. You can pick up an excellent self-guided walking tour of the town and religious complex. The foldout map also has an abundance of information on

the community's past, and lists accommodations—mainly small hotels and bed and breakfasts—including prices and amenities.

Following the walking tour, you'll encounter village squares, pleasant parks, and charming little streets at every turn. The central park, right next to the Great Auditorium, has shade trees, benches, and a dainty gazebo. The main shopping street, Main Avenue, is perpendicular to Ocean Boulevard and is the site of most of the town's dining spots as well.

There's a fine, wide promenade that runs along the ocean-front. Walk down any of the lushly shaded streets and you'll see pastel-colored Victorian houses with lots of gingerbread, turrets, wraparound porches, and striped awnings.

To leave Ocean Grove, take Main Avenue west to the city gates, then turn right onto State 71 after the big sign that reads "God be with you until we meet again."

Drive straight through Asbury Park, once a thriving beach community, which gained fame as the place where Bruce Springsteen's E Street Band got its start. The town is badly depressed now, with many boarded-up buildings and some uninviting-looking motels.

Drive north on Ocean Avenue through Loch Arbour, with its huge mansions and manicured lawns, and the elegant town of Deal, with its huge hedges and towering red squiggle-shaped street lamps.

North of Deal you'll pass through some of the state's northernmost beach towns: Long Branch, a large residential community with idyllic back streets with Victorian architec-ture and mature shade trees, as well as a cluttered commercial zone without charm; Monmouth Beach, given over mostly to high-rises; and Sea Bright, whose massive seawall, condo-minium developments, and beach clubs virtually block the motorists' view of the ocean.

After State 36 crosses the wide mouth of the Shrewsbury River, you'll see signs for Sandy Hook, a windswept peninsula with some fine beaches, great fishing rocks, views out to the Atlantic Ocean, Sandy Hook Bay (which in summer is filled with sailboats), and Raritan Bay.

With the Atlantic to your right and Sandy Hook Bay to your left, the drive to the tip of Sandy Hook is an eerie one along low dunes, great sweeps of grassy sands, and occasional woodsy areas. At the end of the line is Fort Hancock, once a strategically important naval base and now a Coast Guard station and home to Sandy Hook Light, the nation's oldest operating lighthouse. The lighthouse is quite photogenic, though it's rarely open to the public, and the drive around the base, with its stately officers' quarters (now rented out to private and public organizations), is a pleasant one with lots of water views.

Driving back from Sandy Hook point, the tree-filled community you see rising on the hill on the other side of Sandy Hook Bay is Atlantic Highlands, one of Raritan Bay's most affluent residential communities.

But we're not finished with lighthouses yet, for south of Sandy Hook is the Twin Lights Lighthouse State Historic Site. Set on one of the highest points on the Atlantic coast, the beacon was for more than a century the first light mariners saw as they approached New York Harbor after dark.

Getting to the lighthouse can be a bit tricky, so don't hesitate to ask directions along the way if you get confused. Heading south from Sandy Hook, follow the signs for Highlands-Keyport-Route 36 north over the Highlands Bridge. Get into the right-hand lane, and as soon as you get to the other side of the bridge make an immediate right onto the exit ramp (at a sign for the Highlands Business District). Follow the ramp down a steep hill under the Highlands Bridge and bear right onto Highland Avenue, which will take you back up the hill on the other side of the bridge. After passing a condominium development on your left, turn left at the fork onto Lighthouse Road, which will take you directly to the Twin Lights.

The huge brownstone and brick twin towers (which in 1862 replaced earlier lights dating from 1828) were the very first in the United States to be electrically powered (in 1898). Though decommissioned in 1949, the towers still command a magnificent view of Sandy Hook Bay, the Verrazano Narrows Bridge, Staten Island, and, on a good day, Manhattan. A brick path circles the lighthouse and leads out to a scenic overlook where there are park benches for relaxing while enjoying the view. A map at the lookout identifies the land and water masses you are facing. The tower and museum (which has exhibits dealing with navigation, lifesaving, and lighthouse lenses) are open daily from 10:00 A.M. to 5:00 P.M.

Leaving Twin Lights State Historic Site, retrace your drive back to Highlands Bridge and this time follow the signs to State 36 north, which will take you to the Garden State Parkway and points north or south.

If you haven't had your fill of the North Coast, a slew of small roads off State 36 (to the right) lead to quiet old shore towns such as Belford, Port Monmouth, Keansburg, Union Beach, and Keyport, each of which has a distinctly nautical feel. Follow the meandering streets through the towns down to the waterfront, where you'll invariably encounter pleasure boats putt-putting around, fishermen casting in the twilight, and, wherever there's a beach, couples walking hand in hand at dusk watching the sun set over Raritan Bay.

For More Information

Cattus Island County Park (Toms River): 732-270-6960

Island Beach State Park: 732-793-0506

River Belle and *River Queen* party boats (Brielle): 732-528-6620

Brielle Yacht Club Restaurant: 732-528-7000

Sea Crest by the Sea (Spring Lake): 732-449-9031 or
  800-803-9031

The Breakers Hotel (Spring Lake): 732-449-7700

Warren Hotel (Spring Lake): 732-449-8800

Spring Lake Chamber of Commerce: 732-449-0577

D.J.'s Bicycle Shop (Belmar): 732-681-8228

The Normandy (Spring Lake): 732-449-7172

Whispers (Spring Lake): 732-449-3330

Allaire State Park (Farmingdale): 732-938-2371

Ocean Grove: 732-775-0035

Ocean Grove Visitors Bureau: 732-774-1391

The House by the Sea (Ocean Grove): 732-775-2847

Sandy Hook Gateway National Recreation Area: 732-872-0115

Twin Lights Lighthouse State Historic Site (Highlands):
  732-872-1814

Doris and Ed's (Highlands): 732-872-1565

Conover's Bay Head Inn: 732-892-4664

Bayhead Harbor Inn (Bay Head): 732-899-0767

Grenville Hotel (Bay Head): 732-892-3100

Lobster Shanty (Point Pleasant Beach): 732-899-6700

Spike's Fish Market (Point Pleasant Beach): 732-528-7000

Wharfside (Point Pleasant Beach): 732-892-9100

Old Mill Inn (Spring Lake Heights): 732-449-1800

Tyres Bikes (Seaside Park): 732-830-2050

2

Coasting Along the South Shore

Getting there: From eastern New Jersey and New York, pick up the Garden State Parkway to exit 63, then take State 72 east across the Manahawkin Bay Bridge over Barnegat Bay onto Long Beach Island, where the trip begins. From the Philadelphia area, take the Walt Whitman Bridge to U.S. 30 east to State 70 east to State 72 east and across the causeway to Long Beach Island.

Highlights: The state's most popular vacationland—quiet dunes and brash casinos, stately Victorian homes and boardwalk souvenir stands, deserted beaches and the re-created Colonial communities of Smithville and Cold Spring Village.

There's no clear agreement about where New Jersey's North Shore ends and the South Shore begins—so for convenience's sake, we've assigned Barnegat Peninsula and points north to the upper shore area, and everything south of that to the lower shore.

Our three-day excursion takes us from the little resort communities and famous Barnegat Lighthouse of Long Beach Island south to the pretty historic district of fashionable

Beach Haven, the bird-filled
marshes of the Edwin B. Forsythe
National Wildlife Refuge, and into
popular Cape May, New Jersey's Victoriana
capital. Along the way, we'll visit the re-created Colonial village of Smithville, the fifties funtown of
Wildwood, and the Wetlands Institute in Stone Harbor, which
is trying to protect and rehabilitate some of New Jersey's
endangered wetlands species.

If you're planning to go to the beach, be aware that many
of New Jersey's shore communities require beach badges,
which can be purchased at checkpoints along the shorefront.

Beloved by the summer set, Long Beach Island is a world unto
itself. Unlike many other shore resort areas, this former whaling center has a substantial year-round residential population
as well as many summer residents, so there's a real sense of
community up and down the island. Visitors are welcome to
join in, but by and large there's less of the summer business
frenzy found elsewhere at the shore. Certainly, there are some
schlocky sections in several towns where fast-food places,
T-shirt shops, and loud amusement arcades reign supreme,
but Long Beach is more about weathered wood cottages
alongside graceful dunes, quiet villages with Victorian houses,
long stretches of sparkling white sand beaches, and tranquil
wildlife preserves.

Long Beach is 18 miles long and never more than a mile
wide at any point, making for fun exploring on foot or bike
on both the Barnegat Bay and Atlantic Ocean sides of the
island. At many points, the island is so narrow that you can
see both coasts by just turning your head. You can't get lost
exploring the island; its main artery, Long Beach Boulevard,
runs its entire length, with easily navigated side streets in the
wider bulges of land.

Soon after crossing the bridge to Long Beach, pull over at the Southern Ocean County Chamber of Commerce, a few hundred yards ahead on your left. You'll find dozens of pamphlets on places to stay, boating and fishing opportunities, and area attractions. The staff is happy to recommend restaurants and provide up-to-date information about daily events.

Don't be put off by the first sights you'll encounter as you head north on Long Beach Boulevard. The commercial districts of Ship Bottom and Surf City are swaths of ugly shopping strips, outlandish mini-golf courses, and shell shops.

Just keep on driving and soon you'll be in North Beach, where the environment changes completely. Here, pine trees line both sides of the road, with a pretty grass median in the center; many of the houses along the bay and oceanfront are weathered wood and glass affairs, with slanted roofs, skylights, and expansive decks. This is definitely haute beach.

Harvey Cedars, the next town up, is another sweet community with gorgeous views of ocean and bay from Long Beach Boulevard.

In Loveladies you'll see some of Long Beach Island's most interesting architecture—houses in all sorts of shapes combining odd angles and building styles, with rooftop atriums and bubbled skylights lending a decidedly futuristic feel. The reason for Loveladies's extremely modern appearance is that the community was virtually rebuilt after a 1962 storm destroyed almost every house in town.

More down-home, with more traditional beach cottages, is Barnegat Light, the northernmost town on Long Beach Island and home to one of the island's most popular places to mingle with the locals—Mustache Bill's diner. Turn left onto Broadway (there's a sign for the Barnegat Lighthouse); Mustache Bill's is the shiny metal building on your left. This is a classic Jersey diner with lots of chrome on the outside; inside are low

Barnegat Lighthouse on Long Beach Island

stools at the counter and a single row of booths. There's an outdoor dining deck with a bright yellow awning for savoring good weather.

The island ends at Barnegat Lighthouse State Park, home of beautiful Barnegat Lighthouse. Known popularly as Old Barney, it is the second tallest lighthouse in the United States and the most photographed subject at the Jersey Shore. Built in 1856–57, the lighthouse has been guiding vessels along Jersey's dangerous coast ever since, except for a brief period in 1944 when the light was extinguished for fear it would guide German submarines, which were believed to have entered the bay.

Park your car in the large lot and walk up the sandy path to the lighthouse, which sits on a rocky promontory with commanding views of the bay, the ocean, the mainland, and nearby Barnegat Peninsula, which is actually a separate land mass on the other side of a narrow inlet.

For a small admission fee, you can climb the 217 steps to the lighthouse tower. Or, take a stroll along the concrete promenade that juts out along Barnegat Inlet. Even on a sweltering day, the breeze across the walkway is delightfully cooling. As you walk along the promenade, you'll see fishermen casting their lines from the rocky outcroppings adjacent to the walkway, motorboats zooming to and fro in the inlet, and hikers exploring the beautiful sand dunes of Island Beach State Park, at the southern tip of the Barnegat Peninsula.

Heading south from Barnegat Lighthouse via Long Beach Boulevard (also called Central Avenue at the north end of the island), you'll soon pass on your right the Barnegat Lighthouse Museum, open daily from 2:00 to 4:00 P.M. in July and August, and on Saturday and Sunday only in June and September. Set in a former one-room schoolhouse, the museum contains all kinds of lighthouse lore, but it's the outside we found so enjoyable. The Edith Duff Gwinn Garden at the back of the building is a delight of shaded pathways through wildflowers, with benches for resting; birdbaths attract a wide variety of winged visitors. Everything here feels very soft and delicate—a pleasant respite from a busy day sightseeing or lolling on the beach. The garden is accessible even when the museum is closed.

Southbound on Long Beach Boulevard again, we're on our way to Beach Haven, perhaps the island's most interesting town. Here you'll find most of the island's bed and breakfasts, best restaurants, and nightlife. You'll have to pass through the tacky commercial areas of Surf City and Ship Bottom again, but the drive is worth it. At Beach Haven Crest begins street after street of pretty, diminutive beach cottages with sand and pebble front yards, interrupted only occasionally by shopping strips. These are not the tasteful homes of Loveladies and Harvey Cedars—just neat, functional houses for the summer crowd.

Beach Haven has more the feel of a small city than a summer-only retreat. As Long Beach Boulevard passes through the commercial part of town, it becomes Bay Street. At the corner of Bay and Third Streets you'll see 13 newspaper dispensers containing periodicals from Philadelphia to New York and northernmost New Jersey, as well as a few national publications. Beach Haven clearly attracts a cosmopolitan crowd interested in keeping up with the news beyond the island.

The heart and soul of Beach Haven is the historic district, with its many blocks of well-preserved Victorian houses. Your first stop should be the Long Beach Island Historical Association Museum, housed in an old church that sits squarely in the center of the historic district at Engleside and Beach Avenues.

The sprawling two-room museum contains fascinating exhibits tracing the island's glory days as a fishing and whaling center. There's a wall of photographs showing old-time Beach Haven, and several mannequins in historical dress, as well as a changing exhibit (duck decoys were the theme during our visit). Especially interesting are the aerial photos of the terrible 1962 storm that devastated the island, eroding the beaches and washing away scores of houses.

In the museum you can buy a self-guided walking tour of the Beach Haven Historic District covering 52 houses, all built before 1900. Driving up and down the streets around the museum you can see the most interesting houses without ever getting out of your car, but Beach Haven is an enjoyable walking town, so by all means, explore it on foot. There are also wide bike lanes to accommodate bicyclists. You'll no doubt lust a bit after some of the prettiest houses, with their huge wraparound porches, sheltering eaves, and gracious lines.

Across the street from the Historical Museum is the Surflight Theater, where you can catch good theater March through December. Next door to the theater is the island's most popular ice-cream parlor, Show Place, where from Memorial Day through Labor Day college-age waiters sing and dance—often getting patrons to join—in between taking orders.

If your sweet tooth still isn't satisfied, pay a visit to Seafarin' Sweets, located behind Show Place, where you'll find the shore's popular Fralinger saltwater taffy, as well as fudge and other sinful treats.

Below Beach Haven, the dunes get bigger, abutting many of the houses. At the end of the line you can walk past a little swimming beach onto the Holgate Unit of the North Brigantine Natural Area, a 2.5-mile stretch of barrier beach and tidal salt marsh that is a favorite nesting ground for endangered piping plovers (who favor the sheltering dunes) and other waterfowl. The area is closed to the public during the nesting season, from April 1 to August 31.

From the tip of the island you can see the skyline of bustling Atlantic City, but here all is quiet and peaceful.

To leave Long Beach island, head north on Long Beach Boulevard, then take State 72 west over the causeway to the mainland and pick up U.S. 9 south to Tuckerton. (If you're a bird aficionado, take a short detour off U.S. 9 here, following the signs to the left onto Great Bay Boulevard, which will take you out to the bird-rich marshlands of the Great Bay Boulevard Wildlife Management Area.)

Continuing south on U.S. 9 (which briefly merges with the Garden State Parkway), our next stop is historic Smithville Village. Settled in 1787, Smithville was once a stagecoach stop, and the now-restored Smithville Inn was a favored overnight hostelry. When the railroad came, Smithville was bypassed and fell into ruin. In 1949, the Noyes family bought the land and turned the inn into a restaurant. In order to create a historical ambiance that would draw tourists, the Noyeses hauled into town 19th-century South Jersey buildings from elsewhere and restored them into antique stores and other shops. The commercial nature of the enterprise may not please history buffs, but this is a pleasant respite after a long drive, and you can stroll along the boardwalk set over a man-made lake, or rent a paddleboat.

South of Smithville at Oceanville (a pretty, little community filled with gracious old houses), take a drive through the Brigantine Division of the Edwin B. Forsythe National Wildlife Refuge. Follow the sign left at Great Creek Road to the refuge, and be sure to stop at the information booth to pick up a self-guided car tour. The numbered little green ducks in the pamphlet correspond to interpretive signposts along the eight-mile loop through the refuge.

The drive is a pleasant one, under shade trees and across marshlands and through some dense woods, with views of abundant bird life, especially during the fall migration season. The best times to come are sunrise and dusk. In addition to the car route, there are bike paths and walking trails; take some time to pull over and explore more intimately on foot.

Adjacent to the refuge, just off U.S. 9 on Lily Lake Road, is the Noyes Museum, the Jersey Shore's largest fine arts museum. On display here are the works of the state's most talented artists; there's a whole room devoted to waterfowl art, including shorebird decoys.

Back on U.S. 9 south, just before the town of Absecon, State 157 breaks off from U.S. 9. Take State 157 south through pretty Absecon, after which the road merges into County 585 south. (County 585 runs parallel to U.S. 9 but is a prettier route south.) It passes through the old shore communities of Pleasantville, Northfield, Linwood, and Somers Point.

At State 52 follow the signs east toward Ocean City, one of the shore's most popular family resorts, with a fine boardwalk and a clutter of shops and entertainment centers, including a high-rise mini-golf course. The farther south you go, the prettier and less cluttered Ocean City becomes, until it's mainly sand dunes and sweet beach cottages. Follow 55th Street west to County 619 south, which becomes Ocean Drive, a gorgeous route south, also known as the Scenic Route. The road takes you through marshlands and over a small toll bridge across Corson's Inlet, which at dusk is crowded with local fishermen. Gulls swoop low over their heads, hoping to catch discarded fish.

Heading south on County 619 you'll pass through Strathmere, Sea Isle City, and pretty Avalon, all replete with dunes and good beaches.

Soon you'll be in lovely Stone Harbor, a gentrified beach town with a laid-back air. This is an ideal town for bicycling, with lots of quiet streets between Ocean Drive and the beach. It also has a much-respected 21-acre bird sanctuary, located at the southern end of town on Third Avenue between 111th and 117th Streets. During July and August, particularly at dawn, you'll see many herons, ibises, and egrets flying to and from the sanctuary in search of food or a mate.

The Wetlands Institute Detour

A worthwhile detour from the Stone Harbor beach area is the Wetlands Institute, a nonprofit organization bent on protecting and preserving the wetlands ecosystem and educating the public about the delicate balance of nature in the area. To get to the institute, take Stone Harbor Boulevard (also called County 657) west out of town toward the Garden State Parkway. The institute is at 1075 Stone Harbor Boulevard between Stone Harbor and the parkway. Set on a 6,000-acre tract, the institute has a self-guided nature trail with a boardwalk, an observation tower looking out on the expanse of marshes and grasslands (including osprey nesting sights), hands-on exhibits for kids, and a wonderful underwater display of wetlands life. During the summer, there are all sorts of activities, from lectures to birding forays. Every September, the Institute also sponsors a weekend "Wings 'n' Water" Festival with educational and entertaining activities such as boat rides through wetlands, storytelling, and nature walks.

Back in Stone Harbor, be sure to stop at Springer's Ice Cream Parlor at 9420 Third Avenue, where on summer nights folks are lined up for the homemade confection.

Third Avenue takes you south out of Stone Harbor over Grassy Sound, where you'll pick up State 147 east toward the Hereford Inlet and North Wildwood. At First and Central Avenues in North Wildwood, you'll find one of the shore's most treasured lighthouses, the Hereford Inlet Lighthouse, a seven-room Victorian structure built in 1874. The light, whose restoration was paid for entirely with community funds, houses the North Wildwood Tourist Center and Museum. Behind the lighthouse is a pretty garden park. Even when the lighthouse is closed, you can follow the narrow trail beyond the gardens onto the dunes, where benches provide a perch for gazing out on the rocky shoals and the inlet that leads from the Atlantic Ocean to the Intracoastal Waterway linking Maine to Florida.

Continue south on Scenic Drive, through Wildwood's kooky collection of motels left over from the fifties, with Polynesian motifs and other period stylistic touches. Cape May's Mid-Atlantic Center for the Arts (see Cape May) runs Doo-Wop Fifties bus tours through Wildwood several days a week in season. The sounds of Fabian, Johnny Mathis, and Liberace accompany the drive along Atlantic Avenue and other streets where some of the era's most delightfully tacky doo-wop-style remnants—as the locals put it—still survive.

Pacific Avenue south out of town becomes a causeway through marshlands over Jarvis Sound. The stretch over the sound is a strange one with abandoned houses perched on stilts lining the road. These were squatters' cabins that were condemned, turning the alternative community into a kind of floating ghost town.

Head south at the junction with County 109 into Cape May.

Welcome to Cape May, queen of the Jersey Shore and the southernmost town in the state. Favored as a summer resort by the well-heeled set since the 1800s (when folks used to cruise over from Philadelphia along the Delaware River), Cape May boasts the largest concentration of Victorian houses in the nation. Many of these 19th-century gingerbread gems are now bed and breakfasts, a major draw for couples seeking a romantic respite. Fine restaurants, a grand seaside promenade, a historic lighthouse, exceptional birding and whale-watching, miles and miles of quiet farm roads perfect for bicycling (especially Bayshore Road, also known as County 607), and year-round cultural events make this town an always interesting place.

If you have the option, come any time other than summer (or visit midweek in season). The summertime crowds overflow the restaurants, and accommodations can be hard to come by.

Once you get here, park the car for a while and walk the town, strolling along the boardwalk and gazing at the Victorian architecture (Hughes Street, the oldest residential street in town, has some of the finest examples). Then head out of town by car or bike to the natural areas where, even in high summer, crowds are scarce.

Your first stop in town should be the Mid-Atlantic Center for the Arts (MAC) at 1048 Washington Street. Responsible for preserving and promoting Cape May's history and culture, the center has an abundance of free literature encompassing walking tours, Cape May history, and daily doings around town. Housed in the ornate 1879 Emlen Physick mansion, the center runs half-hour narrated trolley tours (for a fee) of the historic area and beachfront—a great way to acquaint yourself with Cape May's highlights. MAC also sponsors a summer music and arts festival, the popular Victorian Week each October, and an old-timey Christmas celebration.

If you're an architecture aficionado, you can spend hours perusing the Victorian houses and identifying their complicated designations, such as "seashore shingle Colonial Revival with gabled roof."

For natural beauty, take Sunset Boulevard (extension of West Perry Street) west of town, following the signs to the 200-acre Cape May Point State Park, site of Cape May's landmark 134-year-old lighthouse. You can walk up the 199-step spiral staircase to the lighthouse tower, follow well-marked trails along boardwalks over the salt marshes, and scout for hawks migrating in season. Cape May is world famous for its concentration of migrating birds each fall. It is the first major peninsula on the East Coast encountered by birds heading south, and many of them pause here before crossing the Delaware Bay, a 13-mile span of water. In season, more species of birds—at last count 402—have been seen in Cape May than anywhere else in North America except southern Texas and southern California.

The waters off the point are also a great place to spot migrating whales and even dolphins.

The public beach here looks out on the remains of a bunker built to keep out the Germans during World War II. Many historians believe that German submarines actually penetrated American waters—and that some were sunk—here, where the Delaware Bay and the Atlantic Ocean meet.

Leaving Cape May Point State Park, turn right onto Lighthouse Drive. At the end of the road, make a right onto Sunset Boulevard. At the first cross street, make a left onto Sea Grove Avenue and follow this to Bayshore Road. Turn left onto Bayshore (County 607), one of the area's loveliest rural routes and a great place to bicycle. As the road winds west you'll pass grazing cows, horse farms, fields of corn, and farmhouses. At New England Road, turn left and follow it to the end, where you'll come upon the Higbee Beach Wildlife Management Area, a 600-acre tract that contains the last natural dune forest along the Delaware Bay shore. The quiet beach abuts woods with hiking trails and is a prime bird-watching site during the migration season, as well as a wonderful place to watch the sunset at any time of year.

Higbee Beach is a fine place to bid farewell to the South Shore. Retracing your way on New England Avenue, cross Bayshore Road and continue on to the canal bridge. Bear right onto County 626 (Seashore Road), which will take you to U.S. 9. Follow the signs to the Garden State Parkway and points north or south.

Cape May–Lewes Ferry Detour

If you've got some extra time, take a ride on the Cape May–Lewes Ferry, a 70-minute mini-cruise (each way) between the shores of New Jersey and Delaware. You can take the car, or go as a foot passenger just to enjoy the ride. The ferry, which leaves from North Cape May, runs year-round.

Historic Cold Spring Village Detour

Three miles north of Cape May off U.S. 9 on Seashore Road is historic Cold Spring Village, a re-created 19th-century South Jersey farm village made up of some 20 old buildings from Cape May County that were saved from razing. The towering shade trees and quiet walkways enhance the stroll through history, and there are demonstrations of early crafts and trades most weekends. During the summer, Cold Spring Village hosts antique shows, craft festivals, and a Saturday night concert series featuring everything from Dixieland to show tunes to symphonic performances.

For More Information

Southern Ocean County Chamber of Commerce
  (Ship Bottom): 609-494-7211

Mustache Bill's Diner (Barnegat Light): 609-494-0155

Barnegat Lighthouse State Park: 609-494-2016

Barnegat Lighthouse Museum: 609-494-2096

Long Beach Island Historical Association Museum
(Beach Haven): 609-492-0700

Surflight Theater (Beach Haven): 609-492-9477

Show Place Ice Cream Parlor (Beach Haven): 609-492-0018

Engleside Inn (Beach Haven): 609-492-1251

Magnolia House (Beach Haven): 609-492-2226

Smithville Village (Smithville): 609-652-2700

Smithville Inn: 609-652-7777

Brigantine Division of the Edwin B. Forsythe National Wildlife
Refuge (Oceanville): 609-652-1665

Noyes Museum (Oceanville): 609-652-8848

Stone Harbor Bird Sanctuary (Stone Harbor): 609-368-5102

Wetlands Institute (Stone Harbor): 609-368-1211

Springer's Ice Cream (Stone Harbor): 609-368-4631

Hereford Inlet Lighthouse and Museum (North Wildwood):
609-522-4520

Doo-Wop Fifties Wildwood Tours (Wildwood): 609-884-5404

Groff's (Wildwood): 609-522-5474

Mid-Atlantic Center for the Arts (Cape May): 609-884-5404

Cape May Point Lighthouse, Cape May Point State Park:
609-884-8656

Cape May Bird Observatory: 609-884-2736

Cape May Whale Watch and Research Center: 609-898-0055

Angel of the Sea Bed and Breakfast (Cape May): 609-884-3369

Captain Mey's Inn (Cape May): 609-884-7793

Chalfonte Hotel (Cape May): 609-884-8409

Mainstay Inn (Cape May): 609-884-8690

Virginia Hotel (Cape May): 609-884-5700

The Washington Inn (Cape May): 609-884-5697

A&J Blue Claw (Cape May): 609-884-5878

The Mad Batter (Cape May): 609-884-5970

Leaming's Run Gardens (Cape May Courthouse):
609-465-5871

Cape May–Lewes Ferry (North Cape May): 609-886-9699

Cold Spring Village (Cold Spring): 609-898-2300

Deauville Inn (Strathmere): 609-263-2080

Harvey Cedars Shellfish Company (Harvey Cedars):
609-494-7112

3

The Pine Barrens

Getting there: From northern New Jersey or New York City, take the New Jersey Turnpike south to exit 4. Take State 73 south for about five miles, then State 70 east to County 541 south at Medford. Follow County 541 to U.S. 206 south. Or, take the Garden State Parkway to exit 67, then County 554 to State 72 west to State 70 west to County 541 south to U.S. 206 south. From the Philadelphia area, take the Benjamin Franklin Bridge to U.S. 30 east to State 38 east to State 70 east to County 541 south to U.S. 206 south.

The trip begins at the Atsion Ranger Station of Wharton State Forest, on your left just after turning south onto U.S. 206.

Highlights: The preserved bog-iron village of Batsto, the cranberry capital of Chatsworth, the blueberry birthplace of Whitesbog, parklands, and the oldest operating winery in the United States.

The Pine Barrens will come as a surprise to people who think of New Jersey as mainly highways and urban malls. Even those who know and love the state's Atlantic coast beaches and Appalachian Trail–crossed northwest hills are often unfamiliar with New Jersey's largest tract of wilderness—covering nearly a quarter of the state.

With 1.1 million acres of pine and oak forest, cedar swamps, and bogs, the Pine Barrens are, in fact, the largest swath of forested land in the nation's northeast corridor between Richmond, Virginia, and Boston. Sprawling through seven counties in southeastern Jersey, just 25 miles from Philadelphia and 30 miles from New York, the region contains the largest unpolluted underground water source in the Northeast—17 trillion gallons in the Cohansey Aquifer. If all that water were brought to the surface, it would cover all of New Jersey 10 feet deep.

Much of the Pinelands—a term preferred by those who point out that the region is anything but "barren"—is dominated by winding rivers and hidden lakes navigable only in small boats, and a crisscrossing network of loose-sand trails maneuverable by only the hardiest four-wheel-drive vehicles.

Through the years, the region's wild looks (including its indigenous species of carnivorous plants) and sometimes eccentric residents have fostered an image of mystery and sinister goings-on. Tales of incest, strange rituals, and unexplained happenings still abound. The most famous legend is of the Jersey Devil, a carnivorous villain with a forked tail, horns, and bat wings who supposedly was the unwanted thirteenth child of a Mrs. Leeds in what's now Leeds Point, or Estellville. The story goes that before the baby's birth in 1735, the mother cursed her pregnancy, and the misshapen monster that emerged from her womb flew out of a window into an adjacent swamp and has been wreaking havoc ever since. Periodic reports of pets disappearing, weird sounds, and unexplained piles of bones discovered in the dense woods keep the devil legend alive, even among some folks who normally would scoff at superstitious hocus-pocus.

To really experience the Pine Barrens, you need to get out of your car and into a canoe, or venture into the woods on foot—avoiding encounters with the Jersey Devil.

Don't expect to find classy—or even quaint—accommodations, gourmet food (except as noted), or great shopping here. Do expect to experience one of the state's last wildernesses—and some unique challenges.

Which brings us to these cautions: there are few signs in the Pine Barrens announcing the beginning or end of any particular town, and many of the smaller roads are either unmarked or labeled with route numbers that are at odds with those listed on maps (county officials are constantly changing route names and numbers), so it's easy to get lost in the area. The Pineys, as residents call themselves, cherish their privacy and seem to like this state of affairs just fine, but in our experience most are happy to provide directions to outsiders, so don't hesitate to ask for help.

Also, many of the routes through the Pine Barrens, though shown on maps as roads, are really just so-called sugar-sand trails. This kind of sand is particularly unstable and gives way easily, much like a dry version of quicksand. Always check with locals (or, better still, rangers) about road conditions before heading down sugar-sand roads in any but the toughest four-wheel-drive vehicle. In winter, a combination of rain, snow, and frigid conditions makes many sugar-sand roads solid, whereas in summer they are prime sinking spots.

As you drive the Pine Barrens, why not get into a folksy state of mind by flipping to the country music station on your radio, or popping a bluegrass tape into the cassette deck. Then again, you might want to time your visit to include a Saturday night, when the Pinelands Cultural Society holds its weekly "Sounds of the Jersey Pines" get-together in the Albert Hall in Waretown. After all, the Pinelands are as much about mood as landmarks.

The Atsion Ranger Station of Wharton State Forest is a good place to get your bearings for your Pine Barrens adventure.

This is one of two offices for the park (the other one is at historic Batsto Village), which is New Jersey's largest state forest—100,000 acres—and the largest tract of public land in the Pine Barrens. The park office has maps and brochures about the area, sells camping permits, if you're so inclined, and provides up-to-the-minute reports on the conditions of the sugar-sand roads. Across U.S. 206, Atsion Public Lake is a refreshing place to stop for a swim (there's an admission charge) in the dog days of summer.

Heading south from the ranger station you'll feel the sensation of getting deeper and deeper into the Pine Barrens—with dwarf pines on your left and taller woods on your right—even though you're on a major road. As you head down U.S. 206, you'll spot lots of intriguing side roads worth a quick jaunt. (County 536, three and a half miles south from the Atsion Ranger Station, is a particularly pretty detour.) Notice the picnic tables set up in the woods just off the road; this makes for a shady break even in the height of the summer heat.

About four miles south of the ranger station, you'll see a sign for Batsto. Turn left, following the sign onto County 613 south. This pretty country road was once a sugar-sand route, but it was paved by Atlantic County to make the historic bog-iron community more easily accessible. This is a gentrified version of the rougher routes, but like them is flanked by scruffy pines, some maples and oaks, and low wild blueberry bushes.

A little more than a mile ahead you'll see another sign to Batsto Village with an arrow pointing left. Make the left onto the unmarked road. You'll pass fields of blueberry bushes and peach and apple orchards on your right, then the Hammonton Municipal Airport on your left. Keep following the signs (which will take you onto County 542 east) to Batsto Historic site and Batsto Village. As at most New Jersey historic and cultural sites, there's a parking fee weekends in season.

Beautifully preserved Batsto was an 18th-century Pine Barrens company town built around the bog-iron industry. In its heyday 1,000 workers lived, worked, and shopped here. The settlement was abandoned after coal was discovered in Pennsylvania in the late 1800s; coal offered a cheaper and higher grade method for smelting iron than Batsto's process of burning pitch pine charcoal.

The village's name came from the word *báatstoo,* an Indian term meaning bathing place; the thermal springs that once flowed beneath the village were considered health promoting.

With its shaded walkways, pretty lake, and woodsy trails, Batsto is a tranquil place given over lovingly to history. There's none of the crass commercialism rampant in many other so-called historic villages. Stroll the shaded grounds, taking a look at the old gristmill and other authentic buildings. In season (check ahead, because the schedule varies) there are guided tours of the grounds, where potters, weavers, candle makers, chair caners, basket makers, and other craftspeople demonstrate old-time skills in little cabins that line the path through town.

Of particular interest is the four-story Italianate villa-style main house with its wraparound porch built in 1784 by William Richards, Batsto's first iron baron. For 92 years, three generations of the Richards family lived in the house and ran the town.

A fire destroyed most of Batsto in 1874, and in 1876 the Richardses sold the house to industrialist Joseph Wharton (of the state forest) for a mere $14,000.

Wharton, who experimented with farming and cattle raising in the area, became notorious for his scheme to extract all of the water from the Pine Barrens area and sell it to Philadelphia and Camden, whose polluted drinking water was causing a typhoid epidemic. Luckily, laws prohibiting export of water were in place by the time Wharton went public with his plan in 1892, and the water stayed in the Pinelands.

Tours through the house, which is furnished with period pieces, though not the building's originals, point out interesting innovations of the time. There's an elaborate bell system connected by wires through the walls that served as a kind of early intercom to summon servants, and warming closets for clothes heated by steam from the chimney. The house also contains a lovely collection of antique dolls and clothing.

Even if no demonstrations or tours are offered during your visit, you could easily spend a few hours exploring the grounds and walking along the well-maintained 1.5-mile nature trail alongside Batsto Lake.

Be sure to take a walk through the spacious visitors center and museum. An airy place, the center has displays tracing Pine Barrens history and ecology from the region's origins as a Leni-Lenape Indian homeland through the years of bog-iron mining, glass manufacturing, and cranberry and blueberry cultivation.

Leaving Batsto, turn right out of the village onto County 542 west heading back the way you came. A little less than a mile from Batsto, turn left at the junction with County 623 and head south toward Sweetwater, a pretty, little community on the banks of the Mullica River—favored by fishermen and canoeists.

The drive is a gorgeous one through woodsy expanses interspersed with simple wooden houses, many of them fronting on the Mullica River. When County 623 south merges with County 643 east, continue straight onto County 643 east.

About one and a half miles down the road, watch for the signs to the Sweetwater Casino, a sprawling bar and restaurant on the banks of the Mullica River. Even if you're not hungry or thirsty, this place is a mandatory stop for its prime location alongside the river. Follow the sign left off County 643 onto the access road to the Sweetwater Casino, then a half mile down turn left into the restaurant's parking lot.

You can smell the heady scent of fresh pine as you walk along the grassy expanse to the big, white Tudor-style restaurant. The broad, open patio, where drinks and snacks are served in summer, is perfect for lazing over a cocktail while watching river life or waiting for your table inside. Catch the whimsical names of some of the cabin cruisers moored in front of the restaurant—*Naked Lady, Sweet Dreams, The Dotty Too.*

The restaurant, an informal place, accepts no reservations, but patrons never seem to mind, since you can spend your waiting time strolling by the river.

Inside, tables lighted by little candles at night are adorned with information place mats containing maps that trace the history of the Pinelands and indicate major sights. The restaurant itself figures into that history. According to local lore, the place is on the site of a former casino (hence the name) notorious for its high-stakes poker games.

After a final walk along the river, head back the way you came to County 643 and turn left onto County 643 east. At the juncture with County 563 continue straight onto County 563 south. About four miles ahead at the junction marked Alt. 561, Smithville, turn left onto County Alt. 561 south, also called Moss Mill Road.

We're headed for the Renault Winery outside Egg Harbor City. Established in 1864, Renault is the oldest continually operating winery in the United States. During Prohibition, the winery made so-called medicinal elixirs, which kept business booming.

Less than a mile down Moss Mill Road (County Alt. 561 south), at the intersection with County 674 north (also called Bremen Avenue), you'll see a big wine barrel and sign for

Renault Winery on your left. Turn left onto County 674 north. The winery is less than a half mile ahead on the right.

Set on a man-made lake with fountains and ducks and outdoor picnic tables, the winery is a pleasant stop whether or not you take a tour. The tour through the facility not only takes you step by step through the wine-making process— culminating with a tasting—but takes you into a little museum area displaying antique wine-making equipment. On weekends, you can eat at the winery's gourmet restaurant, consistently voted one of the most romantic restaurants in New Jersey. There is also a garden café serving soups, quiche, and pasta. Or, buy a bottle of one of the Renault vintages at the winery store and make your own picnic.

After visiting the winery, return the way you came along County 674 (left out of the winery); County Alt. 561 (right onto Moss Mill Road), and County 563 north. At the junction with County 643 bear right, staying on County 563 north and following the sign marked Green Bank, Batsto. A short way ahead you'll cross a bridge over the Mullica River. Make a right immediately after crossing the river, just past the white clapboard building at the end of the bridge, onto the unmarked road along the river. This pretty riverfront lane is River Road, and the short stretch of houses along it overlooks the Mullica River. Though River Road separates the houses from the river, the owners' properties extend to the riverfront, and many residents have set out chaises and little tables along the bank for meals alfresco or after-noon drinks.

Just one-tenth of a mile down River Road, make a left onto an unmarked gravel road. It looks more like a dirt road, but a little more than a half mile ahead it will reconnect with County 563 north on the other side of County 542.

We're bound for Chatsworth, queen of New Jersey's cran-berry trade and the unofficial capital of the Pine Barrens.

County 563 is a woodsy route, ablaze with colors in the fall. To the right and left, you'll see sugar-sand roads leading off into the forest of scrub pine, oak, and maple. These roads are used by hunters, hikers, and hot-rodders out for adventure in all-terrain vehicles. There's rarely much traffic on County 563—mainly cars with canoes strapped to the top and an occasional truck or jeep.

About six miles ahead you'll pass tiny Jenkins chapel on your left—the only indication you're passing through the tiny town of Jenkins Neck. The town is marked on maps, sometimes simply as Jenkins, but, like many so-called towns in the Pine Barrens, its placement on the map is more for the record than for reality. Jenkins Neck is one of many mysterious-sounding Pine Barrens towns whose names certainly must have a story, but it's been lost to history.

County 563 is a good place to rent canoes, as you'll notice from the proliferation of canoe rental places—Mick's Canoe Rentals and Pine Barrens Canoe Rentals among them. The companies usually arrange to shuttle you to a starting point on the nearby Oswego, Mullica, or Wading Rivers, then pick you up at an agreed-upon ending point.

Beyond the canoe rental areas you'll soon pass the region's claim to fame—cranberry bogs. In summer these look like dry swaths of sandy mud with little green sprigs sticking out of them, but in fall when harvesting begins, you'll see ripe red berries floating above the surface as the harvest gets into full swing. October is an opportune time to be here, for the annual Chatsworth Cranberry Festival—a time of bog tours, folk life and song, craft shows, storytelling, and lots of scrumptious cranberry pie, juice, and other berry-based eats.

Notice the squat red cabins on your left; these house the cranberry workers, many of whom are migrant laborers who in season make the region the agricultural version of a company town.

Just beyond the cabins on your left is Chatsworth's pretty, but unmarked, little cemetery. For a break, pull over and take a walk through this final resting place of many of the residents of the 1800s, including a proliferation of Applegates. Looking around at the nearly deserted countryside, you may feel as we did that there seem to be more people in the cemeteries than in the towns.

Just beyond the cemetery you'll pass the Chatsworth Receiving Station of the Ocean Spray Cooperative, where most of the cranberry growers in the area bring their harvest—and share in the profits.

Another short stretch past farms and stone houses will bring you into center city Chatsworth, where County 563 becomes Main Street. During the annual cranberry harvest festival, the town is filled with visitors, but the rest of the year it's just a quiet little residential community, whose "downtown" is dominated by the pretty, white-steepled United Methodist Church on the right and on the left Chatsworth's most famous landmark, Buzby's General Store. Sadly, the eminently authentic store, which dated to 1892, shut its doors in 1997. But it was immortalized in John McPhee's historical account *The Pine Barrens*.

Although by now you have a sense of the Pine Barrens environment, you probably can't appreciate its vastness. For that we're heading for Apple Pie Hill (like Jenkins Neck, the origin of the name is a mystery), just a short drive out of town.

About a block beyond Buzby's General Store, still heading west on County 563, make a left at the firehouse onto Lake Avenue (County 532 west). About one and a half miles ahead on the left are two low brick posts. Make a left between the posts and head down the unmarked dirt road. This is a sugar-sand road, but it's well groomed and you shouldn't have any problems navigating it. The road winds around to the top of a low hill—Apple Pie Hill—to a fire tower. Climb the metal stairs for gorgeous panoramic views of the Pine Barrens. This is a great place to come just before sunset. You'll smell the fresh scent of pine as you look out on miles and miles of pine trees broken by the narrow traces of sugar-sand trails.

Retrace the sugar-sand road back to Lake Avenue (County 532), turn right onto County 532 east heading back toward Chatsworth, then turn left onto County 563 north. The drive through the heart of the Pine Barrens is beautifully woodsy, with mile after mile of pine, oak, and maple. A little less than four miles ahead, County 563 merges with State 72. Bear left onto State 72 west, a wide artery. About two and a half miles ahead on the right is the headquarters for Lebanon State Forest, the second-largest Pine Barrens public park after Wharton State Forest. This office tends to be short on maps and informative literature. The only reason to stop by is to check directions or book campsites within the Lebanon Forest confines.

Just beyond the Lebanon State Forest Headquarters at the intersection with State 70 (one of New Jersey's main east-west arteries), turn right onto State 70 east. Though a major highway, State 70 retains a Pine Barrens flavor, with trees dominating the landscape on both sides. About seven miles ahead turn left onto County 530 at a sign for Browns Mills and Fort Dix. Notice the cranberry bogs on your right and left. A little more than a mile ahead turn right at the little sign for Lebanon State Forest and Whitesbog Village.

Whereas Chatsworth is associated mainly with the cranberry business, Whitesbog is prime blueberry turf (though it is surrounded by cranberry bogs as well). It was in Whitesbog that one Elizabeth White, eldest daughter of a cranberry farmer, first succeeded in cultivating the wild blueberry in 1916 with the help of Frederick Covell, a scientist from the U.S. Department of Agriculture.

The 19th-century village, once the center of the White family's cranberry and blueberry business, has been maintained by the Whitesbog Trust. Several of the original workers' cabins and family houses still remain; the site is also headquarters for the Pinelands Institute, which promotes Pine Barrens education programs and organizes guided walks of the area.

In July each year, the village is the site of the Whitesbog Blueberry Festival, a wonderful country fair with musical performances, craft sales, and food stalls selling all things blueberry—from blueberry pies and bagels to blueberry bushes and even blueberry-motif napkins and greeting cards. Best about the festival, however, are the guided bus and walking tours, which take in the flora and fauna of the area, including, of course, the blueberry and cranberry farms.

In October, Whitesbog has a cranberry harvest festival—not as big as Chatsworth's, but fun nonetheless. Unless your visit coincides with a festival or one of the nature walks organized by the Pinelands Institute or Whitesbog Trust, you're on your own here.

Park in the large lot and, after exploring the village, take a stroll down the dirt track (to your right when facing the administration building), which leads through woods filled with wild blueberry bushes to a vast network of cranberry bogs.

The area abounds with bird life. If you've come in autumn, you may be lucky enough to arrive as cranberries are being harvested. These bogs, which are old, hand-dug pits, are much less efficient than more modern bog operations. They are harvested the old-fashioned way, with migrant workers, many of them Asian immigrants, wading waist deep in the water, "herding" the floating cranberries with lengths of rubber tubing. Modern cranberry farms have giant tractorlike vehicles with big rubber wheels and scoopers to do this exhausting work.

By the way, you can drive this route as well, but it's more fun on foot. The walk along the rough sand tracts between the cranberry bogs is a peaceful way to greet the dusk; you'll seldom encounter more than a handful of other visitors.

After exploring the bogs, return to the parking lot and leave Whitesbog the way you came, returning to County 530 (east this time) and then turning left onto State 70 east.

Our last stop in the Pine Barrens is Double Trouble State Park, a 19th-century logging center with a preserved sawmill, remnants of the old logging village, a one-room schoolhouse circa 1890, and a lovely 1.5-mile marked nature trail around an old cranberry bog, a cedar swamp, and stands of magnolia, mountain laurel, and pitch pine.

The route to Double Trouble is a bit complicated, so follow directions carefully. Taking State 70 east, five miles ahead turn right at the sign marked 530/539, Forked River. At the sign for County 530 east, bear left toward Forked River. The road, a pretty, winding one that snakes through several towns, changes names several times, becoming Lacey Road, then Pinewald-Keswick Road. At the intersection with Dover Road (there's a stoplight), continue straight, crossing Dover Road. (Do not turn left onto County 530 east). The entrance to Double Trouble State Park is about two and a half miles ahead on your right, past the state police and the municipal building for Berkeley Township. (Do not turn in at the canoe ramp, which comes up first.)

After exploring the village buildings, head for the nature trail (to your left after you pass the entrance gate). Pick up a guide map from the box at the trail entrance. The trail is an easy, flat, straightforward one, and the numbered items in the guide, which correspond to numbered posts along the route, explain quite a bit about the history of cranberry cultivation.

The industry began as a way to make use of the depressions in the land caused by the removal of bog iron in the late 18th and early 19th centuries. The cleared land, which was loamy and acidic, and the readily available water proved ideal for cranberry production.

The nature walk around an old cranberry bog and through woods and swamplands is particularly enjoyable at sunset, and can be accomplished leisurely in less than an hour. There couldn't be a more mellow way of ending your Pine Barrens excursion.

Turn right out of Double Trouble, where signs will direct you east to the Garden State Parkway and points north or south.

Getting to Know the Pine Barrens with an Expert

Bill Leap, a Runnemede naturalist and historian, runs day-long car caravan tours through the ghost towns of the Pine Barrens, stopping along the way to talk about the history, life, and lore of the area, its heroes and villains, and quirky tall tales. You drive your own car, following Leap along unmarked (but sturdy) sugar-sand roads you'd never be able to navigate on your own and stopping for a picnic lunch along Lake Oswego. Leap's tours, usually run only in May and October, are a wonderful way to get a feel for the region before you go exploring on your own. He skips the more touristed sights, such as Batsto Village and Chatsworth, figuring that visitors can easily explore those places on their own. For information, write Bill Leap, 1 Washington Avenue, Runnemede, New Jersey 08078, or call 609-939-1856.

Finding accommodations in the Pine Barrens is very difficult. Unless you want to camp (in which case, inquire at one of the park headquarters below), you'll likely have to bed down outside the area at one of the inns, or in Medford, Hammonton, or Manahawkin.

For More Information

New Jersey Pinelands Commission (New Lisbon): 609-894-9342

The Albert Music Hall's "Sounds of the Jersey Pines" (Waretown): 609-971-1593

Atsion Ranger Station, Wharton State Forest: 609-268-0444

Batsto Village: 609-561-3262

Sweetwater Casino: 609-965-3285

Renault Winery (Egg Harbor): 609-965-2111

Renault Winery Restaurant (Egg Harbor): 609-965-2111

Mick's Canoe Rentals (Chatsworth): 609-726-1380

Pine Barrens Canoe Rentals (Chatsworth): 609-726-1515

Chatsworth Cranberry Festival: 609-859-9701

Lebanon State Forest (New Lisbon): 609-726-1191

Whitesbog Village (Browns Mills): 609-893-4646

Double Trouble State Park (Bayville): 908-341-6662

Braddock's Tavern (Medford Village): 609-654-1604

Maplewood Inn (Hammonton): 609-561-9621

Ramada Inn (Hammonton): 609-561-5700

Goose & Berry Inn (Manahawkin): 609-597-6350

Red Lion Motel (Southampton): 609-859-3488

4

Exploring the
Southwestern Bulge

Getting there: From North or South Jersey, take the New Jersey Turnpike to exit 3, then State 168 north to I-295 south to State 42 south to State 55 south to exit 26, Wheaton Village. From Philadelphia, take the Walt Whitman Bridge to State 42 south to State 55 south to exit 26, Wheaton Village.

Highlights: Coves, marshlands, and winding rivers, tranquil communities, a glass museum, antique shopping, ancient Indian shell mounds, paddleboat tours, and the famous Cowtown Rodeo.

When most people think of South Jersey, they think of bustling beach resorts with seaside boardwalks and crowded sands. Few tourists know anything about the state's quiet southwest, a lovely expanse of coves, marshlands, and winding rivers along the Delaware Bay, and tranquil communities with nautical pasts boasting gracious Victorian houses and sparkling white churches. This weekend journey takes us to the state's so-called southwestern bulge. Starting in Millville's Wheaton Village, site of a wonderful glass museum, we'll head down toward the mouth of the

Maurice River, a prime spot for watching the shorebird migration each spring and snow geese each winter, then up to Mauricetown, a venerable old sea captain's village. Farther west we'll explore the bayside community of Fortescue, where fishing charters can be arranged, then proceed to the architecturally rich communities of Bridgeton, Greenwich, and Salem, finishing up with antique shopping in Mullica Hill and a Saturday night at Sharptown's Cowtown Rodeo.

A word of warning: this part of the state has a profusion of roads and routes with constantly changing names and numbers. At this writing, the names are all accurate, but we advise double-checking directions as you leave a town bound for another one; by all means, stop and ask for help whenever you're unsure of your next step.

Set on the outskirts of the glassmaking community of Millville—one of the oldest glassmaking communities in the state—Wheaton Village is a re-creation of an 1880s South Jersey glass-manufacturing town. The village brings the area's past to life with demonstrations of glassblowing as well as other period crafts, such as pottery making, decoy carving, and lamp working. The Wheaton Museum of American Glass on the grounds houses one of the world's largest collections of American glass, with 7,500 objects on display. There's blown glass, pounded glass, etched glass, and melted glass. There's an entire case of decorative paperweights through the decades, fine examples of the works of Steuben and Tiffany, and even an exhibit of Thermos bottles showing how a vacuum bottle works. Even those who wouldn't know Depression glass from carnival glass (both favored by collectors) will enjoy looking at all the different kinds and colors produced through the years.

The C. P. Huntington, a half-scale replica of an 1863 locomotive, makes a three-quarter-mile scenic trip around the village grounds (the cost of the train is included in the village entrance fee), with a stop at The Country Inn, a lakeside hotel in Wheaton Village.

Of course the true heart and soul of the region is the Delaware Bay—our next stop. From Wheaton Village, take State 55 south to State 47 south (Delsea Drive) past Leesburg to County 740 south, which turns into County 616 south (Heislerville-Leesburg Road).

At the dead end, turn right onto East Point Road and follow this to the end. Here you'll see the bright red East Point Lighthouse, on a little bluff just up from the beach at the mouth of the Maurice River where it meets the Delaware Bay.

The light was originally operated by whale oil when it was built in 1834, then switched over to kerosene in 1860, then decommissioned after World War II, when commerce on the Maurice River waned. The lighthouse was recently restored as a historic site by volunteers from local historical societies, and is the only example remaining of a long string of lighthouses that once protected seamen in the Delaware Bay.

The sand at the river's mouth is an amazing sight each spring (mainly in April and May), when millions of horseshoe crabs come up the Delaware Bay to lay billions of eggs, which line the beach to a depth of a foot or more. What makes the sight even more dramatic is that this annual egg laying coincides with the annual northern migration of millions of shorebirds bound for arctic nesting sites from South America. Winging over the Atlantic Flyway with stomachs empty and fat burned from their long flight, they descend on the crab eggs, using the beach as a refueling stop before continuing north. The sight draws scores of bird-watchers, who flock to the area to watch the annual feeding frenzy. The area is also a prime spot for viewing snow geese migrating south in January through March.

Many of the sandy mounds you'll see in the marshes as you drive around the area are actually ancient shell mounds that date from the region's earliest Native American inhabitants.

During the 19th century, sea captains often navigated their three-masted schooners from the bay up the river, mooring them at our next stop—Mauricetown. The famed freshwater port was free of the barnacles that would have formed on vessels' bottoms in the salty sea harbors, and the captains built gracious seaside estates where they could come home to roost—and keep an eye on their ships.

Leaving East Point Light, take East Point Road back the way you came and turn left onto County 616 north (Heislerville-Leesburg Road), following the road along the water through Leesburg and Dorchester. At State 47 turn left and follow this to the light at County 670. Turn left and cross the bridge over the Maurice River into Mauricetown. Turn left at the first street, Front Street (County 744), which will take you into the center of town.

Mauricetown (pronounced Morristown) looks like a New England village transplanted to South Jersey. From 1810 to 1910 some 80 sea captains lived in 45 Victorian and gingerbread houses in town. Many of the restored houses have plaques with dates identifying their earliest occupants, who often passed down their houses to later generations of sea captains. The spire of the sparkling white United Methodist Church (built in 1880) at Second and Noble Streets was once used as a navigational aid. Stained glass windows on the second floor of the church bear the names of 21 men who never returned from the sea.

Now a quiet bedroom community (many of the residents commute to jobs in Philadelphia), the town has a plethora of white-shingled houses, gardens, vibrant green lawns, gazebos, and antique and collectible shops. The very active historical society sponsors an annual house tour in December, and the fire department runs several antique shows throughout the year. A statewide oyster-shucking contest held each October during the annual seafood festival draws visitors from around the state and nearby Pennsylvania.

It's fun just to randomly navigate the tiny town (the main streets are Front and High). Every turn reveals a stately mansion or a diminutive cottage painted in pastel shades—sometimes matching the flowers in the gardens.

For a basic reconnoiter follow Front Street to Noble Street and turn right. The high-spired church at Noble and Second Streets is the aforementioned United Methodist Church, with the seamen's names in stained glass on the second floor. The church is usually open, so head upstairs and take a look. Then, turn left on Second Street. The house on your left at the dead end at South Street is the Caesar Hoskins log cabin, the renovated home of Mauricetown's first settler, a Swedish schooner operator. A carved sign on the door reads 1650.

A left turn onto South Street brings you back to Front Street. Turn left on Front. At High Street, a right turn takes you to Mauricetown Riverfront Park, where you can picnic overlooking the Maurice River and the remnant of an old swing drawbridge dating from 1888. Returning on High past Front, you'll pass through town, past the Greek Revival Mauricetown Academy. Built in 1860, this was a two-room elementary school and was an educational institution for 100 years before becoming the town's community center.

Leaving Mauricetown, continue on High Street (County 676) west out of town through Haleyville, where the road dead-ends at County 553 at Dividing Creek. Turn right onto County 553 west. This rural route, which passes along farmlands and small town centers and over little creeks, is the main thoroughfare through this part of the Delaware Bay region.

If you're feeling adventurous, make a left turn when you reach the town of Newport. Follow the signs to the bay town of Fortescue, following County 732 and County 637 through the marshlands down to the water, where you can get great views of the bay and boat life. At the harbor, you can charter a fishing boat for half or full-day outings. Sitting on the banks of the bay watching the gulls swoop low, it's hard to believe that this quiet world so far removed from the Atlantic Ocean resorts is also the Jersey Shore. Even at the height of summer, you may have to share the view with only a few locals.

If you wish to skip that excursion, then from County 553 west, follow the signs to Bridgeton, where you'll pass several more quiet Delaware Bay towns. One of the prettiest is Cedarville, which has a dramatic town church with a peaked steeple and a big lake filled with ducks. Stay on County 553 as you go through Fairton, then follow the signs to Bridgeton, which will put you on County 609 (South Avenue) into town.

Now the presiding river is the Cohansey—once, like the Maurice River, a vital shipping route to the Delaware Bay. These days, the Cohansey's attraction is to pleasure boaters and visitors to the river-hugging towns of Fairton, Greenwich, and Bridgeton.

Originally a riverside sawmill town and shipping center, and later the center of the state's nail manufacturing trade, Bridgeton is struggling hard to come back from an economic slump following the decline of its most recent industries: food processing and glass manufacturing. Some of the downtown area still looks down at the heels, but Bridgeton has quite a bit to offer visitors: a landscaped waterfront promenade, summer paddleboat tours along the Cohansey River with live ragtime music; and a 1,200-acre wooded park with a zoo, a large lake, canoe rentals, a re-created Swedish village honoring the area's original settlers, and a museum that shows the history of the town's once booming nail industry.

Bridgeton is most famous, however, for its historic district—the largest in New Jersey—with some 2,200 homes and commercial buildings on the National Register of Historic Places. The Colonial, Federalist, and Victorian gems reach back some 300 years. Each year just before Thanksgiving, there's a holiday house tour in which a trolley shuttles people throughout the historic area.

At the Bridgeton Tourist Office, which is housed in a former railroad station, you can pick up a free walking tour map of the historic district as well as self-guided audio tour tapes for rent. Coming into town on County 609 (South Avenue) you'll pass right by the tourist office at the intersection with State 49 (Broad Street), where County 609 becomes State 77.

The main part of the historic district begins at the juncture of Commerce Street (the town's main thoroughfare) and Mayor Aitken Drive. The prettiest houses line both sides of Lake Street. (Heading west on Commerce, turn right on Giles Street, which dead-ends at Lake.) To really savor the area, park your car on Lake and explore on foot.

Perhaps the most famous building in town is Potter's Tavern (51 W. Broad Street), a small wooden edifice dating to 1773. Here the state's first newspaper, the *Plain Dealer,* a broadsheet that advocated independence for the colonies, was published weekly between Christmas 1775 and March 1776. Friday through Sunday, visitors can tour the tavern, which has been restored and furnished to an 18th-century look.

The Old Broad Street Church, at West Avenue and Broad Street, has never had electricity—and still doesn't—so all activities are carried out during the day, with candles providing the only illumination.

A quirky side note to Bridgeton's history is its name. The city's original name was Bridge Town. When the first bank opened here in 1816, the name was misspelled "Bridgeton" on the bank stationery and building plaques, and it was cheaper to change the name of the town to the misspelled version than to have the signs and stationery redone!

Dealt a happier fate by history is the tidewater town of Greenwich (pronounced phonetically), considered perhaps the prettiest town on the Cohansey.

To get to Greenwich from Bridgeton, follow West Commerce Street past the historic district. Turn left onto West Avenue, then right onto County 607, a lovely drive alongside peach orchards and farm country. County 607 dead-ends at Ye Greate Street, Greenwich's main thoroughfare.

The town was laid out in 1685 by John Fenwick, the English Quaker who founded Salem. Ye Greate Street is great indeed—100 feet wide and lined with huge shade trees and 17th- to 19th-century buildings, many of which have been lovingly preserved and labeled with their historical roots.

Turn left onto Ye Greate Street. Immediately on your left stands the Greenwich Post Office, which shares a building with the Greenwich Country Store—the only food emporium in town.

About half a block down at Market Lane you'll come to a monument commemorating the town's most famous event. In 1774, a group of young patriots held their version of the Boston Tea Party. Disguised as Indians, they stole a load of tea from a British merchant; instead of dumping it in the river, as was done in Boston the year before, they burned it in a public bonfire in the center of town as a protest against unjust taxation.

Ye Greate Street is lined with wonderful old houses. Beyond the tea burners' monument, you'll pass the Friends Meetinghouse and burial ground dating to 1771, before the street dead-ends at a housing development. Return the way you came on Ye Greate Street. For a relaxing lunch, turn left on Market Lane and follow it to the river, where the Ship John Inn offers dining overlooking the Cohansey.

Back on Ye Greate Street, continue west past the intersection with County 607, and several houses down you'll see a sign for the Cumberland County Historical Society. Ensconced in the Gibbon House, whose namesake was a ship owner and merchant, the historical society has displays of period furniture, clothing, and children's toys. The society also publishes a self-guided walking tour of town and arranges guided tours. The annual Christmas house tour is a highlight of the year. The society is open Tuesday through Saturday and closed January through March. Heading west out of town on Ye Greate Street (also called County 623), keep an eye out for the 1728 Old Stone Tavern (at Bacon's Neck Road), the oldest tavern in the country, which once offered—as a plaque indicates—"bedde and board for man and beast."

Farther on you'll pass a little stone schoolhouse on your left. Endowed in 1810 as a free school for poor children by one Zachariah Barrow, it's the oldest educational building in Cumberland County and was a beacon of hope for poor families until the advent of public-supported learning.

You'll hardly know you've left Greenwich and entered neighboring Othello—you're still on Ye Greate Street, still flanked by gorgeous shade trees. Soon you'll be in a rural world of woods and farmlands, where groups of children fish from the banks of creeks against a backdrop of doe-eyed grazing cows.

Farther along, in Canton (you'll see a general store with a big sign for LAC—Lower Alloway Creek), bear left at the fork onto Harmersville Road (County 658), which will take you through more farmlands into Hancocks Bridge along Alloway Creek, which empties into the Delaware Bay. The town was the site of a bloody massacre in the early morning hours of March 12, 1778, when 30 American rebels garrisoned in the home of Judge William Hancock were bayoneted to death, along with Hancock, by British troops.

Coming out of Hancocks Bridge, Harmersville Road becomes Salem–Hancocks Bridge Road, but is still County 658. Five miles north on County 658 you'll come to Salem, perhaps southwestern Jersey's most famous town thanks to its landmark 500-year-old, 80-foot-high, 30-foot-wide oak. To get to the Salem Oak, which sits majestically in the Friends Burial Grounds, turn left off County 658 onto Broadway (State 49). The burial ground is about a block past Market Street on your right. A plaque describes how the oak marks the spot where Salem's founder, John Fenwick, made a peace treaty with the Leni-Lenape Indians in 1675.

Legend has it that another famous event happened in 1820. Judge Robert Gibbon Johnson stood on the steps of the Salem Courthouse at Broadway and Market Streets and publicly ate the first Jersey tomato, which he had grown in his garden, to prove it wasn't poisonous, thereby starting an industry that still thrives today. Historians dispute the story, claiming that the tomato was around long before Johnson, but the tomato tale remains as embedded in Salem lore as the oak is in its soil.

A good place to start a walking tour is at the Salem County Historical Society, in the 1721 Alexander Grant House at 79–83 Market Street, just north of the intersection with Broadway. The Grant House is also a 20-room museum of period furnishings and artifacts from Colonial times to the mid-19th century.

Pick up the latest copy of the historical society's open house guide (there's a much publicized house tour every other year in May) for a detailed description of some of the most important homes, many of which date to the early 18th century. The area north of the historical society around Market Street (also called State 45), East Broadway, Hancock Street, and Howell Street is filled with classic saltbox houses and Victorian cottages with lots of gingerbread trim, beveled glass, and expansive porches and gardens.

Sadly, the urban renewal of the 1960s knocked down many of the old houses, but the historical society has been busy renovating the substantial number still standing.

A lovely place to stay in the area—as well as an important part of Salem history—is Abbotts Bed and Breakfast at Tide Mill Farm, home to five generations of the Abbott family, whose descendant, George, founded Abbott Dairies in 1876. Once one of the largest dairies on the East Coast, the dairy shut down in the 1960s, but the Abbotts are still there. After one of her hearty breakfasts, proprietor Emaline Abbott will be happy to show you around the old plantation house and tree-shaded grounds, pointing out old dairy museum pieces. She'll also show you the kitchen steps that lead down to a cistern where the Abbotts' Quaker ancestors hid slaves heading north as part of their flight to freedom along the Underground Railroad.

To get to Abbotts Bed and Breakfast, take Market Street (State 45) north from center city Salem. About a mile after crossing Fenwick Creek and after passing Mannington Mills, turn left at Tide Mill Road (across from a large building labeled ARC). Tide Mill Road dead-ends at the Abbotts.

Heading north from the Abbotts on State 45, the road soon forks (at the Memorial Hospital of Salem County). Take the middle fork onto County 620, which is the historic Kings Highway (also called the Pointers-Swedesboro Road). This Colonial thoroughfare was one of the original "corduroy roads," so-called because the logs laid down to make the roadbed over the muddy earth gave the appearance of corduroy. The roads were used by stagecoaches and horses bound for points north in New Jersey and Philadelphia. The old "highway" goes all the way to Haddonfield, where it disappears into the suburbs. In this part of Jersey, Kings Highway is just one very narrow lane in each direction that passes through gorgeous farmlands and planted fields, small rural communities, and marshlands filled with all manner of bird life—a pleasant alternative to other more congested routes east and west.

As you come into the old Colonial village of Sharptown, notice the little graveyard on your left and the church beyond it. Along the roadside stands one of the last old mile markers from the original Kings Highway.

At the intersection with U.S. 40, stop for a break at Richmond's Ice Cream Company, an old ice-cream factory and dairy that dishes out some of the best homemade ice cream around.

If you're in the area on a Saturday evening between Memorial Day and Labor Day, you're in luck. Just a half mile west on U.S. 40 is the Cowtown Rodeo, a professional operation that the Harris family has run weekly each summer since 1955. Beginning at 7:30 P.M. as many as 3,700 folks from all over the region come to sit in the bleachers and cheer on their favorites at bareback bronco riding, calf roping, steer wrestling, brahma bull riding, team calf roping, and women's barrel racing. After the rodeo, head west a few miles on U.S. 40 to the Friendly Tavern (U.S. 40 and Courses Landing), where you'll likely run into many of the cowpokes kicking up their heels to country and western music at the tavern or at its adjacent annex, The Little Cabin.

Tuesday and Saturday from 8:00 A.M. to 4:00 P.M., a giant flea market on the rodeo grounds draws as many as 40,000 bargain hunters.

Back on Kings Highway (County 620), continue north about eight miles, crossing a railroad track into Swedesboro, a charming residential town settled by Swedish colonists about 1620. Townsfolk still treasure the memory of a visit by Swedish King Carl Gustav VI in 1976 during the Bicentennial celebration, when he paid homage to his ancestors with a stop at the 1784 Trinity Episcopal "Old Swedes" Church, a Georgian structure at 208 Kings Highway.

A walk down Kings Highway, Swedesboro's main street, leads past many architecturally significant houses, some restored, others in need of work. One standout is the Old Swedes Inn, at 301 Kings Highway, a salmon-colored Victorian mansion that is now a popular restaurant open for dinner nightly and lunch Tuesday through Sunday.

At the corner of Kings Highway (now County 551) and County 538 stands Stratton Hall, birthplace in 1796 of Charles Stratton, the first elected governor of New Jersey in 1845.

If you're a shopper, you're probably getting itchy at the end of this long weekend of mainly visual and historical appeal. Never fear. Our last stop is Mullica Hill, a well-preserved Colonial community settled by Finns and Swedes that's now an antiquing mecca. Coming out of Swedesboro, continue north on Kings Highway (still County 551) to the intersection with U.S. 322. Turn right onto U.S. 322 and proceed to State 45, and you'll be in Mullica Hill.

Antique lovers from all over New Jersey, Pennsylvania, Delaware, and Maryland converge here (many in chartered buses) to shop along an approximately five-block section of Main Street (State 45). Dozens of stores—from plain spaces crowded with secondhand books and old doll pieces, to elegantly appointed shops with fine furniture and art priced in the stratosphere—sit side by side, some in single buildings, others sharing large barnlike enclosures. At The Old Mill, some 30 stores are clustered on three floors. Some folks will consider the wares great finds; others will see them as material for the trash heap. Regardless, it's fun to browse through history here. No doubt you'll come upon some dolls, appliances, or old newspapers that will bring back memories.

Pick up a map of Mullica Hill antique, collectible and specialty shops, available at many stores in town.

Before leaving the area, you can buy Jersey corn and fresh peaches in season (they're sold all along State 45). Then you're homeward bound—take State 45 north to U.S. 322 east, then take the New Jersey Turnpike to points north or south.

For More Information

Wheaton Museum of American Glass (Millville): 609-825-6800

The Country Inn at Wheaton Village (Millville): 609-825-3100

Mauricetown Historical Society: 609-785-0457

Fortescue Captain and Boat Owners Association (fishing charters): 609-447-5115

Bridgeton Tourist Office: 609-451-4802

Bridgeton Pleasure Boat Company (canoe rentals): 609-451-8687

Benjamin's (Bridgeton): 609-451-6449

Jersey Cow Cafe (Bridgeton): 609-455-8791

Greenwich Country Store: 609-453-1871

Ship John Inn (Greenwich): 609-451-1444

Bacon's Grant Bed and Breakfast Inn (Greenwich): 609-453-9537

Cumberland County Historical Society (Gibbstown): 609-455-4055

Salem County Historical Society: 609-935-5004

Abbotts Bed and Breakfast at Tide Mill Farm (Salem): 609-447-4928

Brown's Historic Home Bed and Breakfast (Salem): 609-935-8595

Richmond's Ice Cream Company (Woodstown): 609-769-0356

Cowtown Rodeo (Sharptown): 609-769-3200

Friendly Tavern (Penns Grove): 609-299-1222

The Little Cabin (Penns Grove): 609-769-1222

Mullica Hill Merchants' Association: 609-478-0010

Harrison House Diner (Mullica Hill): 609-478-6077

J. G. Cook's Riverview Inn (Pennsville): 609-678-3700

Josiah Reeves House (Alloway): 609-935-5640

5

Quakers and Sea Life
Around Camden

Getting there: From northern New Jersey and the New York City area, take the New Jersey Turnpike to exit 5 and follow County 541 north to Burlington. From the downtown Philadelphia area take I-95 north to U.S. 13 north to State 413 south across the Burlington-Bristol Bridge to Burlington.

Highlights: Quaint small towns, Camden's waterfront and aquarium, the Cafe Gallery, a Quaker meetinghouse, farm stands, picturesque Victorian homes, American Revolution battle sites, and the Walt Whitman Museum.

This trip takes us to Walt Whitman's home and grave in Camden. On the way, we travel along the west side of the state and the Delaware River, to quaint small towns such as Burlington, and past old, faded warehouses—into the heart of the beauty that puts the "garden" in the Garden State, and the grit that gives New Jersey its down-to-earth, urban reputation. And we'll visit the Camden waterfront, which is undergoing a revival, including the wonderful Camden Aquarium. While traveling, remember these words from Whitman:

63

Allons! whoever you are come travel with me!
Traveling with me you find what never tires.

Listen! I will be honest with you,
I do not offer the old, smooth prizes, but offer rough new
prizes,
These are the days that must happen to you.

—Walt Whitman
"Song of the Open Road," from *Leaves of Grass*

Burlington is surrounded by cornfields: this part of New Jersey grows enormous amounts of the corn and tomatoes for which the state is known. High Street is the town's main thoroughfare. The classic Burlington Diner, like a fifties postcard, glows chrome and neon at the corner of U.S. 130 and High Street. Continue past it a half mile or so to a row of small historic houses. The Pearson-Howe House, at 453 High Street, is the oldest, built in 1705 and enlarged in 1740, and furnished with early 18th-century antiques. At 457 High Street is the James Fenimore Cooper House, and next door to that is the Lawrence House, where James Lawrence was born in 1781. Lawrence was the young naval commander who, during the War of 1812, coined the phrase "Don't give up the ship." The houses, maintained under the auspices of the Burlington County Historical Society, are open Sunday through Thursday.

Historic buildings abound in town, with the greatest concentration on High, Union, and Broad Streets. The historical society has an informative map of some of the most significant, including what it claims may be the oldest building in Burlington County—the Revell House, on Wood Street, built in 1685. It's sometimes referred to as the Gingerbread House, because Benjamin Franklin supposedly ate some gingerbread there on his way to Philadelphia.

The "downtown" area has colorful and well-kept stores in buildings boasting their age and heritage in the brickwork. Refreshingly noncommercial are an ice-cream parlor, a little antique mall, Flora's First Choice Thrift Shoppe, a barbershop with a faded barber pole, a McCrory's five-and-dime, and little delicatessens with fountain service. The Burlington Pharmacy (1731), at 301 High Street, is said to be the oldest continuously operated pharmacy in the country, and was a center for antislavery activity.

At the end of High Street, you can park for free and enjoy the riverside park and its promenade, with a bandstand for music in the summer and views of the Delaware and Burlington Island. In 1624, Europeans established the first settlement in the state on this island. The first murders in New Jersey were here, too, when two Indians killed two Dutchmen.

From the park you can walk to Burlington's popular eating establishment, the Cafe Gallery. It is, indeed, both café and gallery, serving French cuisine amid airy rooms filled with art; upstairs is a separate gallery with changing exhibits. The restaurant has a good Sunday brunch; ask for a table by the window and spend the morning watching the river roll by.

Burlington was settled by Quakers in 1677 and is full of Quaker influence. The Quaker Meetinghouse, set back on High Street, is still in use after 200 years. Walk behind the building to the Quaker cemetery, notable for several reasons. At the front is the grave of Chief Ockanickon, a friend of the early settlers; his grave bears the advice: "Be fair and plain to all, both Indian and Christian, as I have been." The graves here are modest, the dates expressed as "second day of the second month," to avoid worldly artifice. Some graves bear only a name. Walk through the cemetery and cross the street to two adjoining cemeteries, in the old and new St. Mary's churches. Note the evolution of grave markings, from simple to elaborate. The newest of the churches includes the graves of Bishop William Henry Odenheimer and Lt. Col. William

Bradford, attorney general under Washington, as well as other luminaries.

Leave Burlington on High Street, returning to U.S. 130 south; travel three miles and exit the highway past the sign for Edgewater Park (Wood Lane). At the end of the street, turn left onto Warren Avenue; you'll drive past some wonderful old houses. Curve left into the town of Beverly; now you'll be on Burlington Avenue. On Lilac Street, turn right and head toward the Delaware River, then turn left at the end of Lilac onto Delaware Avenue. You'll pass some glorious houses, well situated with views of the water. Soon the road ends and you have to turn left onto Willow Street. Follow Willow, which bears to the right and goes right onto Burlington Avenue.

You'll pass the old Watchcase Tower, reminiscent of the area's manufacturing heyday. At the big crossroads, turn right and follow the railroad tracks. Keep your eyes peeled for Taylor Avenue, a dirt road on your right, and turn onto it. At a half mile you'll see a sign for Taylor's Wildlife Preserve—Walkers Welcome. Follow the signs to the small farm stand in front of the Taylors' farmhouse. Joseph Taylor, whose family has owned this farm since 1720, passed away, but his wife, Sylvia, and her son, Harold, continue to work the farm, growing "a little bit of everything," as Sylvia says, from peas in May to pumpkins in October. From the farm stand, you can continue down the rutted road, right through the fields of squash, corn, and eggplant, into the State of New Jersey Natural Lands Trust Preserve. Park at the end of the road, where you can pick up hiking trails that will take you along the river or into the swamps on the property. It's quiet, remote, and fairly wild.

Haddonfield is our next destination, via some pretty roads and past some interesting vistas. Retrace your way on the road through the preserve, bearing right at the fork; at times, water from the swamp comes right up to the road. Continue to River Road, and turn right.

Turn left at the light in Riverton onto Main Street and proceed down the pretty, tree-lined road past houses with big porches, and past the Cinnaminson High School. Main Street turns into Riverton Road; cross U.S. 130 and continue along Riverton Road as the road widens and heads into the woods. Soon you'll be in Moorestown, where a sign at the entrance to town warns: "Hunters must register with police." Many houses are built right into the forest, and more immense ones are rising.

Riverton becomes Chester Avenue at the first stoplight in Moorestown. Proceed straight at the light. Two lights ahead at the T, turn right onto Main Street. Half a block down on the right, the First Fidelity Bank sits on a site formerly occupied by an 1800s tavern and then a stagecoach stop where well-to-do people overnighted on their way to New York or Philadelphia. Next to the bank is Friends' Cemetery, where the first Friends' meetinghouse was built in 1700; the log structure is gone now, but there is a brick meetinghouse across the street, built in 1802. Main Street is lined with historic buildings with plaques explaining their heritage.

Heading west out of town on Main Street, you'll pass picturesque Victorian houses. Keep left at the fork onto Kings Highway, the prettiest stretch of road in the area. Continue to Strawbridge Park on your left. The park has a large, lily pad–strewn pond that falls decorously over a small drop; in fine weather, people bring their lawn chairs and sun themselves on the wide lawns, as families of ducks waddle by.

Stay on Kings Highway into Haddonfield; at the circle, keep following the highway (State 41 south).

Haddonfield was founded in 1713 by Elizabeth Haddon Estaugh, and the current residents have done a good job of preserving the past; the town is both a state and national historic district, including 488 houses. Kings Highway runs through the downtown of attractive stores, galleries, and antique shops. Self-guided walking tour pamphlets are available in many stores. You'll also pass the Indian King Tavern Museum at 233 Kings Highway. The building has been everything from museum to statehouse; New Jersey's seal was adopted here in 1777.

Also on the highway is the Historical Society of Haddonfield, in the Georgian-style Greenfield Hall at 343 Kings Highway East, and the Haddon Fire Company, one of the oldest in the country, at Haddon Avenue; the latter has a small museum.

Turn right onto West End, which is lined with more lovely homes. When Kings Highway ends, turn left and take U.S. 130 south. Stay to the right and follow the signs to National Park, County 642. At the stop sign turn right onto Hessian Avenue.

Hessian Avenue is lined with basic suburban houses, but during the American Revolution it was filled with Continental soldiers who appropriated the home of James and Ann Whitall. From the bluffs overlooking the Delaware, they defended the strategic area against the British, who had already gone into Philadelphia, just across the river, and had warships crossing the Delaware.

On October 22, 1777, 2,000 Hessians attempted a sneak attack on the 400 soldiers still making ready for battle. Miraculously, the minority won out, partly because they were alerted to the plot. The land attack was over in half an hour, with 500 Hessian casualties to the 14 Americans killed. The battle on the sea raged for another day, during which a cannonball flew through the roof of the Whitall House, where Ann was spinning wool. She is said to have calmly picked up her wheel and moved to the basement.

The Red Bank Battlefield site was taken over by the federal government, so the optimistic townfolk decided to name their place National Park. The federal government turned it over to the county, which still operates it as a historic site. Visitors can tour the Whitall home and walk the grounds, where you can still see the trenches and the started fort. You can walk down to the river along a paved path; there are several seating areas. You may want to time your visit for sunset; many of the locals set up camp here just to watch the sky turn colors over Philadelphia across the water.

Although Camden is teetering on the verge of a renaissance, you shouldn't wander around many parts of the city at night. If you do reach Red Bank Battlefield at sunset, save Camden and the aquarium for the next morning, and head for Maple Shade or Cherry Hill, both rife with lodging possibilities.

You'll want to get onto U.S. 130 north (the road out of the park will take you there), which goes into Camden, feeding directly into the newly rebuilt Camden waterfront. There's an indoor parking garage across from the aquarium, and outdoor metered parking to the left, by the marina (housing and an arts center are planned for this area).

The $52 million aquarium opened in February 1992 and is home to more than 4,000 aquatic animals, including African penguins in its new Inguza Island exhibit. The aquarium underwent a $4 million renovation in 1996, adding the Ocean Base Atlantic theme, with more than 1,000 new and colorful fish.

The 760,000-gallon Open Ocean tank is set up like a giant movie screen in an amphitheater where you can watch sharks—and the divers who feed them. Using underwater microphones, the divers can even answer questions, such as whether they've ever been bitten by one of the sharks in the tank. (The answer, so far, is no.) Similarly large in scope, the entire side of the building facing the river is glass, reminding visitors that water is all around us.

The aquarium is small enough not to feel overwhelming

or cause children to get restless. There are lots of hands-on activities for kids, including a touch pool with baby sharks and skates and other marine creatures, watchfully supervised by staff. The aquarium's 200-seat auditorium features live performances as well as films. There's a big gift shop, and a pleasant outdoor Riverfront Cafe with beautiful views.

The enormous crowds that heralded the aquarium's debut have mercifully dwindled, but you should arrive early in the day so you won't feel harried.

The promenade on the waterfront is pleasant for a stroll; from here, you can pick up the Riverbus, which every half hour takes a 10-minute ride to and from Penn's Landing in Philadelphia, at reasonable rates.

To the northeast of the aquarium is the new General Electric complex, part of which occupies the old RCA Victor building on Market Street. It's worth a stroll to gaze up at the familiar Victor lettering above the doorway, and the clock tower, whose faces are adorned with stained glass reproductions of none other than Nipper the dog. Camden's waterfront revitalization has also brought the Sony Blockbuster Entertainment Center, and a $5 million Children's Garden Theme Park is in the works. Campbell's Soup headquarters is just north of the aquarium.

When you leave the aquarium, continue straight on Mickle Street, a wide, sullen road. Pass the YMCA, and across from the prison you'll see a row of unassuming brick and clapboard buildings on the right. Walt Whitman lived at Number 328 in the last years of his life.

Whitman lived the life of his poetry: adventurously but simply. This was the only house he ever owned; he had little furniture—just his pipe and slippers and some clothes. Most of the furniture was owned by Mary Davis, a woman who came to live with him as his housekeeper. He paid $1,750 for the house in 1884—about twice what it was worth. No one is quite sure why.

Most days, few people come to visit the museum, which is really a shrine to the man and the poet. Douglas Winterich, historic preservation specialist and your guide through the house, can tell you as much as you want to know about Whitman (as much as can be known, since he burned a lot of his personal papers); you may learn, for instance, that he became furious if anyone touched his papers. He would sit in his favorite chair—a Christmas present from the children of some close friends—surrounded by papers, piles three feet high everywhere. Winterich has the photographs to prove it. The humble abode was visited by everyone from John Burroughs to various British royalty. A special reception is held every May 31, Whitman's birthday.

The neighborhood here looks seedy, but there's a police station across the street, and parking directly in front of the museum, we have been assured, is safe. Across the street, in front of the prison, watch for a minute on the sidewalk and you'll notice a curious phenomenon. Relatives and friends of the inmates have developed their own sign language to communicate with the people behind the windows. They're there through rain, snow, and brutal heat.

To continue the Whitman theme, proceed down Mickle Street, through three traffic lights; at the third turn right onto Hadden Avenue. Go about two miles, passing dilapidated row houses, the Dr. Martin Luther King Community Center, the Camden Study Group for Louis Farrakhan, the imposing Our Lady of Lourdes Medical Center, and the turnoff for the Camden County Historical Society on Vesper Street, and you'll arrive at Harleigh Cemetery. Turn left at the entrance and you'll see two signs—one pointing to Whitman's grave to the left, the other to haiku poet Nick Virgilio's grave to the right.

Go left just a short way and you'll see a mausoleum nestled in the shade of the trees on your left. The cemetery gave the plot to Whitman, and he paid for the mausoleum, where his mother and brother are also buried. There's a black granite monument with the Great Gray Poet's likeness on it, and his words:

> I bequeath myself to the dirt to grow from the grass I love,
> If you want me again look for me under your boot soles.

The cemetery is full of picturesque mausoleums, and in the center is a pond. In summer, children may be found leaping into the water, dousing themselves against the urban heat. Whitman probably would have liked that. Overlooking the lake, too, is Virgilio's grave, with a lectern bearing his famous poem: "Lily / out of the water / out of itself."

To stretch your legs on some walking trails, head for the New Jersey Audubon Rancocas Nature Center. But first . . . go left at the gate and bear left at the light, following the signs to U.S. 130 north. Stay on U.S. 130 as it curves back and forth, past the fast-food places and gas stations, and follow the sign to Merchantville. You'll be on Maple Avenue, with big old houses set back on expansive lawns. Continue straight after the traffic circle, where you'll find more enormous houses.

Maple Avenue hooks up with Kings Highway; you'll pass by the Perkins Art Center in a small park jutting between two roadways. Stay on County 537, past more elaborate homes and the General Electric Aerospace Center. Go right under the train trestle and continue on County 537, which becomes a rural, two-lane road cutting though cornfields and taking you into Mount Holly, site of the Battle of Iron Works Hill on December 23, 1776. At the Robin's Nest Bakery and Cafe, turn left onto High Street. There's an old prison-turned-museum just down High Street on the left. The prison was designed in 1808 by Robert Mills, a noted Federal-style architect whose plans still influence penal buildings. Keys and chains surround the "Prison" sign on the building's facade.

High Street abounds with grand old historic houses that have been turned into lawyer's offices. Drive down to Front Street and turn around.

Take County 537 to County 541 bypass to Rancocas Road. A mile outside of Mount Holly you're in—Timbuctoo! Nothing to see, but you can say you've been there. Continue another nine-tenths of a mile to the entrance on the left for the New Jersey Audubon Rancocas Nature Center, where the Audubon Society has set up a 130-acre preserve. Pick up a trail guide at the center and walk the one-kilometer loop, taking in 200 kinds of plants and lots of birds.

Farther down Rancocas Road is the entrance to Rancocas State Park; this section is the Powhatan Renape Nation, Rancocas Indian Reservation, with an American Indian Heritage Museum open on Saturday or by appointment.

To return home, turn right out of the visitors center, then left onto County 431 to the New Jersey Turnpike, and points north and south.

For More Information

Burlington Diner: 609-387-0658

Burlington County Historical Society: 609-386-4773

Cafe Gallery (Burlington): 609-386-6150

Smith Cadbury Mansion, Historical Society of Moorestown (Moorestown): 609-235-0353

Indian King Tavern Museum (Haddonfield): 609-429-6792

Historical Society of Haddonfield: 609-429-7375

Queen Anne Inn (Haddonfield): 609-428-2195 or
    800-269-0014

Red Bank Battlefield (National Park): 609-853-5120 or
  609-468-0100

New Jersey State Aquarium (Camden): 609-365-3300

Walt Whitman House (Camden): 609-964-5383

Walt Whitman Cultural Arts Center (Camden): 609-964-8300

Camden County Historical Society: 609-964-3333

Pomona Hall, Camden County Historical Society:
  609-964-3333

Harleigh Cemetery (Camden): 609-963-0122

Riverbus (Camden): 609-365-1400 or 800-634-4027

Stedman Art Gallery, Rutgers University (Camden):
  609-757-6245

New Jersey Audubon Rancocas Nature Center
  (Rancocas Woods): 609-261-2495

American Indian Heritage Museum (Rancocas Woods):
  609-261-4747

Beau Rivage Restaurant (Medford): 609-983-1999

Braddock's Tavern (Medford): 609-654-1604

Clayton's (Mariton): 609-985-5585

Olga's Diner and Pastry Shoppe (Mariton): 609-596-1700

Barclay Farmstead Museum (Cherry Hill): 609-795-6225

Cherry Hill Mall (Cherry Hill): 609-662-7440

Delaware River Region Tourism Council and the Greater Cherry
  Hill Convention and Visitors Bureau (Cherry Hill):
  609-482-2828 or 800-355-2828

Ponzio's Restaurant and Bake Shop (Cherry Hill):
609-428-4808

Feather Nest Inn (Cherry Hill): 609-663-0411

Inn of the Dove (Cherry Hill): 609-488-2323

Clementon Lake Amusement Park (Clementon): 609-783-0263

Ristorante Gina Rose (Voorhees): 609-751-5454

6

From Pitch Pines
to Princeton

Getting there: Take the Garden State Parkway to exit 120. Curve around the exit off the parkway, and turn right at the stop sign. At the light a half mile ahead, turn right onto Cliffwood Avenue; .8 mile farther, turn right onto Gordon, which leads through suburbia into Cheesequake State Park. From the Philadelphia area, take the New Jersey Turnpike to the Garden State Parkway and onward.

Highlights: Cheesequake State Park, historic farms and museums, horses and barns, grand old homes, well-preserved towns, the mother of all flea markets, historic Princeton, canoeing on the canal, and two-stepping.

This weekend, we can commune with nature or bargain with flea market vendors, get reflective, get refined, or get rowdy. This weekend we run the gamut of emotions and activities as we traverse the state from east to west, from the edge of the sea to the hallowed halls of Princeton.

We'll visit one of the state's loveliest parks—Cheesequake State Park—tour historic farms and museums, and have a

honey of a time in Colts Neck, courtesy of
the local beekeeper. We'll pass horses and
barns and grand old homes, wend our way
through tiny, well-preserved towns, take a
paddle on the Delaware & Raritan Canal,

and wind up doing a bit of two-stepping in Manville.

You'll need three nights to do this trip right; you should
spend at least one of them in Princeton to make even a dent in
its list of attractions.

Nobody's quite sure what the word *Cheesequake* means,
although the people who know such things agree that it's an
old Leni-Lenape Indian word. So visitors must remain in the
dark, etymologically speaking. But many other mysteries of
nature will be revealed in Cheesequake State Park, especially
if you take the 3.5-mile Green Trail—the longest of three hiking trails in the area. In 90 minutes, you can traverse every
type of terrain found in New Jersey: white cedar swamps,
200-year-old pine groves, oak forests, mountain laurel glens,
and woods with the ubiquitous pitch pines of the Pine Barrens, tulip poplars, and more. Boardwalks carry hikers over
the swampiest, frog-laden parts, and benches have been
installed for thinking, or for stealing a kiss from your honey.

The 1,274-acre park also has plenty of areas for bicycling
and picnicking, the six-acre Hooks Creek Lake for swimming
(no boating, though) and ice skating in winter, and wonderful
expanses of fields for romping with your dog or tossing a Fris-
bee. A modern Interpretive Center, complete with a stream
and exhibits on other habitats in the area, is nestled into the
forest along the Red Trail; the site is handicapped-accessible
via an unpaved road leading up to a parking lot and a boardwalk path to the door.

After your visit to Cheesequake, return to the Garden State
Parkway and head south into Monmouth County. Continue

for about 11 miles to exit 109, Lincroft; turn right after you exit and head toward Lincroft and the Monmouth Museum. Another one and a half miles ahead, turn left into Brookdale Community College and follow the signs to the museum; park in the lot across the road.

The small museum presents a wide array of exhibits each year, from paintings to crafts to tapestries, plus a holiday exhibit. There's a Children's Wing with all sorts of activities. The gift shop is wonderful for children's items, from marionettes to books and games.

Turn left at the college exit, back onto Newman Springs Road, which passes pretty Thompson Park and gets more pastoral, with white-fenced pastureland on the right and forest on the left. About a mile down the road, turn right onto Crawfords Corners Road, which passes farms and farm stands. In about three miles a strange white water tower will appear on the horizon. The aliens haven't landed; it's just part of Bell Labs, coming up on your left. A sign near the road indicates that on this site in 1932, Bell scientist Karl Jansky first discovered radio waves from space.

In another half mile turn left onto Roberts Road, then turn right onto Longstreet Road. Just past the sunflowers and the cows, turn left into Holmdel Park.

This is a well-used park, and a favorite among parents, who like to introduce their young ones to the lambs and the chickens at historic Longstreet Farm. The working farm and farmhouse are just one aspect of this 340-acre park, which also includes an arboretum, hiking trails, a shelter and concession stand, and playgrounds.

On most weekends at the 19th-century farm you can see park employees in period costume performing chores. The 14-room Victorian farmhouse is open on most weekends for tours; there's no admission to the farm, but there is a fee to tour the farmhouse.

Less than a minute north on Longstreet Road, you can go even farther back in time at the Holmes-Hendrickson House (open May through October), where, for a small fee, you can have an extremely thorough look at life in the 18th century. The house, one of five owned by the Monmouth County Historical Society, is an unusual mix of English and Dutch styles. The two groups didn't like each other much when they first settled the area. But love is blind, so Englishman William Holmes built a house incorporating many Dutch elements to please his new Dutch bride.

Though William Holmes was well-off, his house evidenced staunch farmer—and Dutch—pragmatism. No marble fireplaces, no whitewashed walls, rush instead of fabric chair seats (everything would get too dirty, what with the smoke from the fireplaces and the grime of the fields). The Holmeses had 11 children; it must have gotten pretty crowded in there.

Your tour guide will point out the mix of styles: Dutch doors, a grand hall (British), detailed woodworking in a British linen storage hutch, and elegant simplicity in a Dutch *kas,* or armoire.

Upstairs you can learn about the work and crafts of the era in rooms given over to farming equipment, quilting, spinning, and weaving. The demonstrations are hands-on; kids love playing with the curly wool from just-shorn sheep (courtesy of Longstreet Farm).

When you leave, turn right and go back down Longstreet Road, bearing right at the fork and continuing down this road, which feeds into State 34. The street is literally draped in greenery so dense that the ivy is hanging from the trees.

Be on the lookout for Brock Farm Garden World on your left; actually, you can't miss it. In the fall, the place is covered with Halloween ornaments, and there's a haunted house out back; in winter, the workers funnel their spirit into Christmas displays.

About four miles from Holmdel, turn right onto County 537 into Colts Neck and the center of town, such as it is. On your right is the sleepy Colts Neck General Store; turn left into the driveway across the street and pull behind the red-shingled building. Here you'll find the Colts Neck Honey Shop.

You may be the only one there besides proprietor and beekeeper Harry Barth, who might just come out to meet you and personally welcome you to his shop. Inside the small store, which smells like honey and may hum vaguely with a bee or two, the walls are lined with jars and plastic bears filled with the sweet stuff. Barth and his bees make most of the honey on hand, from blueberry to tulip poplar flavors. He's got hand-dipped beeswax candles, beeswax soap, beeswax sculptures, and lots of literature on bees. Barth has had the store since 1972; he also hires out as an expert at removing pesky bees' nests from people's homes. If you ask, he may show you some of the enormous hives he's conquered. He's quite used to bee stings, and in the course of a chat may transport an errant apian quite gingerly by the wings to the out-of-doors. But even he has had his memorable bee moments; ask him about the bee in his ear.

Continue on County 537, past classic white houses with columns and the Hominy Hill Golf Course, past State 18 into Freehold Township. Freehold is sedate and reserved. A succession of large houses with sweeping porches are set back on the tree-lined main street. Freehold, formerly Monmouth Courthouse, is the county seat. At the grand House of Records, a cream-colored building with black shutters, turn right onto Court Street. You'll immediately begin passing one heart-stoppingly beautiful house after another. Most are occupied by lawyers. Two blocks down on the left, at 70 Court Street, is a surprisingly new (1930), albeit stately, building housing the Monmouth County Historical Association Museum and Library. Along with its changing Monmouth-related exhibits, the small museum has a few pieces of note-worthy antique furniture, a collection of charming primitive paintings by local artist Micah Williams, and a Discovery Room for kids, where they can dress up in Colonial costumes, play old-fashioned games, try their hand at old-style penmanship, peek into a little Victorian house, and heft a gun shell from the Battle of Monmouth.

The library, housing resources on Monmouth County's history and genealogy, requires a separate admission fee. The museum is closed Monday; the library is closed Monday and Tuesday.

Across the street from the museum, on a triangle of land, is the Monmouth Battle Monument; for more information on the battle, continue the way you were headed on Main Street, where, in fine weather, outdoor cafés are set up along the sidewalk. Turn onto State 33 west (toward Hightstown), and after the Freehold Raceway Mall, exit at Wemrock Road. Pass Wemrock Orchards and turn left at the light toward Monmouth Battlefield State Park, about 1,000 feet ahead on your right.

The visitors center has numerous displays and recordings telling the tale of the battle—the only one in the American Revolution in which both commanding generals (George Washington and Sir Henry Clinton) went head to head. After a rough winter at Valley Forge, the Continental army was hoping to flex its muscle, show what it had learned, and resist the British who were on their way from Philadelphia to New York via Sandy Hook. This they did on June 28, 1777, as the British made ready to leave.

Also in the park, on County 522, is a reproduction of the Molly Pitcher well, from which the patriotic woman supposedly brought water to the soldiers during the battle. You can also tour the 1710 Craig House, taken over by the British during the battle. The house is open weekends in summer and by appointment in winter.

Unlike some battlefield sites, Monmouth is a rather festive one. There's fishing, two picnic areas with a playground, a concession selling ice cream and other snacks, and cross-country skiing in winter. The park has 25 miles of hiking trails.

An especially interesting feature of the park is Owl Haven, a nature center run by the New Jersey Audubon Society. To get there, turn left at the exit to the park, left at the first light, and left at the stop sign. Watch for the sign about a mile down on the right.

The center is run by Alice Forshee, who obviously cares deeply about the animals in her charge, which include a variety of turtles, snakes, and, when we visited, a screech owl and a kestrel, both unfit to be released into the wild. Forshee keeps the birds at home in large cages but usually brings them to work with her, so you can visit with them, too. The 1,520-acre haven has hiking trails, and guided walks are offered periodically.

Englishtown Flea Market Detour

The mother of all flea markets is the Englishtown Auction Market. To get there, continue along County 522 from Monmouth Battlefield State Park until the road ends at Main Street. Turn right and continue through town, bearing left onto Wilson Avenue, which becomes Old Bridge–Englishtown Road (County 527). The flea market looms large on your right. There's paid parking close to the action, or free parking at the edge of the market. Englishtown is not as authentic as it once was; although the farmers still sell produce of all sorts, most of the merchandise for sale is new—"plastic" as one old-timer put it. Still, up to 10,000 people may shop here on a

Saturday or Sunday; those in the know arrive very early to snatch up the best stuff.

Our next stop is Cranbury—one of the quaintest towns in New Jersey. To get there, return to County 522 by turning right on Main Street and left at the light onto Water Street. Continue onto Wood Street, which is County 522. About three miles out of town, the road gets more rural; at four miles you'll see Farmer Al's, where you can pick your own vegetables in season. In another mile, you'll go through Jamesburg, then back out into farmland. In two and six-tenths miles, turn left onto County 535 south, passing an odd mix of cornfields, industrial parks, and farm stands. The road curves sharply left and right, but just keep following the signs for County 535 toward Cranbury.

Cranbury is an old-timey kind of place where children careen down the sidewalks on bikes and folks sit on their front porches talking for hours with neighbors and visitors. Most of the houses are white, with lots of gingerbread trim. Main Street is a few blocks of stores all starting with Cranbury: Cranbury Bookworm, Cranbury Collectibles, Cranbury Market.

To get to Main Street, bear right at the fork coming into town, turn right onto Plainsboro-Cranbury Road, then turn left onto Main Street. To reach the village park, at Scott Avenue turn left. One block ahead turn left again onto Maplewood Avenue. The entrance to the quiet park, with its lake and gazebo, will come up on your right. Park in the lot and explore for a while. If it's Sunday, save time to visit the Cranbury Museum: as you leave the park, turn left onto Maplewood, then right onto Park Place; the museum, home of the town's historical society (open Sunday only), is on your left.

Leaving town on Main Street, you'll pass the firehouse (the old mill site), the town's history center, and The Cranbury Inn; turn right onto Cranbury Neck Road and pro-

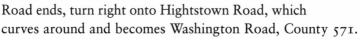

ceed through flat fields of crops and more vegetable stands. Go over a small metal bridge and continue through Graver's Mill (site of Orson Welles's radio broadcast about the fictional War of the Worlds) to Princeton Junction. When Cranbury Road ends, turn right onto Hightstown Road, which curves around and becomes Washington Road, County 571.

Continue around the circle, following the signs to Princeton. The road stretches majestically in front of you, lined by stately elm trees forming an arch—a fitting entrance.

Everything about Princeton is prim and proper and grand, from the glorious old mansions to the plethora of historic buildings to the magnificent campus to the mix of preppy stores and student-oriented eateries on Nassau Street. The signs for the shops on Palmer Square are done in Norman Rockwell style, completing the good-old-days scene.

Princeton has so much to see and do that you could spend days here. If you have the time, by all means take a room at the historic Nassau Inn on Palmer Square, dating from 1757, and let Princeton unfold over time. If you don't have long to spend, you'll have to choose what appeals to you most and vow to come back another weekend.

You can feel the pulse of the town along Nassau Street, which you'll find by following the signs to the business district. Park anywhere along Nassau or the square; you'll need to feed the meters until 6:00 P.M. daily except Sunday. Maps of the town can be purchased at the newsstand at Palmer and Nassau. Doff your cap to the bronze fellow perpetually reading near the kiosk.

Take a walk around Palmer Square, with its litany of upscale shops: Sealfon's, Crabtree & Evelyn, Laura Ashley, Ann Taylor. Even if you don't stay at the Nassau Inn, you might consider a meal or a drink there. Palmer's restaurant is rather elegant, but if you're not dressed for a big to-do, head for the more casual Tap Room. The walls are lined with photographs of venerable sports teams and famous graduates. One of the thousands of Princeton traditions is to carve your name into the battered tables. Don't miss Norman Rockwell's *Yankee Doodle Dandy* mural, the biggest picture he ever painted.

Behind Palmer Square, and down Greenview Street, is Princeton Cemetery, a veritable Who's Who of American history. Among those buried here are Aaron Burr, Jr. and Sr., Jonathan Edwards, John Witherspoon, and Grover Cleveland. Maps are available at the superintendent's house near the entrance.

Return to Nassau Street and enter the Princeton University campus through the wrought-iron FitzRandolph Gates, built in 1905 by the prestigious architectural firm of McKim, Mead and White and named after Nathaniel FitzRandolph, who gave the land on which Nassau Hall stands.

You can get a map of the campus from one of the guards at the drive-in entrance. You'll be surrounded by important-looking buildings, and there's a lot to see: the templelike Whig and Clio halls; the castlelike Blair Hall; Picasso's *Head of a Woman* sculpture at the entrance to the Art Museum (worth touring); the famous pair of bronze tigers; the soaring University Chapel; and the football player sculptures on various buildings, most notably Dillon Gymnasium. The college offers hour-long tours daily except Sunday, beginning at the McLean House on Nassau Street.

The Historical Society of Princeton, in Bainbridge House on Nassau Street, offers a walk through history on weekends.

Princeton University began as the College of New Jersey in 1753, when it moved from Newark. The college and the town have grown together. The college has also affected the world, educating such influential people as James Madison, Woodrow Wilson, many senators, and, of course, Brooke

Nassau Hall, Princeton University

Shields. Albert Einstein, Thomas Mann, and Paul Tulane hobnobbed here. Princeton abounds with houses of the rich and famous: Einstein (112 Mercer Street), John F. Kennedy (on the campus, at 9 South Reunion Hall), F. Scott Fitzgerald (15 University Place and 51 Prospect Avenue), Robert Oppenheimer (97 Olden Lane), and Paul Robeson (110 Witherspoon, but it didn't have aluminum siding when he lived there).

When the Continental Congress, nervous that the soldiers would be angry for not getting paid, had to beat a hasty retreat in 1783, they ensconced themselves in Nassau Hall, at the time the biggest building in the country.

Speaking of soldiers, the Battle of Princeton was, obviously, fought here. Take Nassau Street west out of town (it becomes Stockton Street), and you'll pass the Princeton Battle Monument, which is followed by Springdale College; Morven, the Georgian mansion of Richard Stockton; and Drumthwacket, the governor's mansion (tours are offered on Wednesdays). Take the first left onto Quaker Road, and then a second left onto Princeton Pike. Spreading out on either side of the road is Princeton Battlefield State Park, where, on January 3, 1777, General Washington gained a strategic victory over General Charles Cornwallis with a surprise attack.

Preserved and protected on the battlefield site is a spreading oak tree where Gen. Hugh Mercer lay after he was wounded, refusing to be taken away until he was sure that his army would be victorious.

We'll never be on our way if we don't stop thinking about Princeton, so return toward the town proper and turn left at Nassau Street and immediately right onto U.S. 206 north to Rocky Hill Borough. At the Montgomery Shopping Center turn right onto Franklin Turnpike. Take the turnpike over the Delaware & Raritan Canal, then turn left onto Canal Road, which follows the water and skims the Delaware & Raritan Canal State Park.

The 64-mile canal connecting the Delaware and Raritan Rivers was built in the early 1830s mainly to transport coal from Philadelphia to New York. At one point in 1871 it was busier than New York's Erie Canal.

Today the canal is a lot more peaceful, though it occasionally rings with the sounds of laughter and splashing as someone falls or is pushed out of a canoe into the stream; canoe rental companies include Griggstown Canoes on Canal Road. The towpath has been turned into a jogging and bicycling path. The canal is listed on the National Register of Historic Places.

You can also follow a path into the woods and down to Stony Brook. Or visit the restored Mule-tender's Barracks next to the canal and the canoe launch site in Griggstown, open on Sunday only.

A little history, a little paddling—what more could you want? How about a little two-stepping?

Cross over the canal to its western bank in Griggstown, and turn right onto County 533, River Road, through historic Millstone into Manville. On the right at the light you'll see a large parking lot, which fills with cars Tuesday through Saturday nights, as cowboys and gals hightail it to the Yellow Rose for tireless two-stepping and Texas waltzing. The western outfits are as entertaining as the band.

A night of stompin' on the dance floor ought to get your adrenaline flowing for the ride back home. Saddle up your horsepower and take County 533 north to I-287, which connects with I-80 and the New Jersey Turnpike and points north and south.

For More Information

Cheesequake State Park (Matawan): 732-566-2161

The Monmouth Museum, Brookdale Community College (Lincroft): 732-747-2266

Holmdel Park (Holmdel): 732-946-2669

Longstreet Farm (Holmdel): 732-842-3758

Holmes-Hendrickson House (Holmdel): 732-462-1466

Colts Neck Honey Shop (Colts Neck): 732-462-0937

Colts Neck Inn (Colts Neck): 732-462-0383

The Monmouth County Historical Association Museum and
Library (Freehold): 732-462-1466

Monmouth Battlefield State Park (Freehold): 732-462-9616

Owl Haven (Freehold): 732-780-7007

Monmouth County Tourism (Freehold): 732-431-7576

Englishtown Auction Sales (Englishtown): 732-446-9644

The Nassau Inn (Princeton): 609-921-7500

Tap Room (Princeton): 609-921-7500

Historical Society of Princeton (Princeton): 609-921-6748

Thomas Clarke House, Princeton Battlefield Park (Princeton):
609-921-0074

McCarter Theatre (Princeton): 609-683-8000

Princeton Area Convention and Visitors Bureau (Princeton):
609-683-1760

Alchemist and Barrister (Princeton): 609-924-5555

Mexican Village (Princeton): 609-924-5143

Peacock Inn (Princeton): 609-924-1707

P.J.'s Pancake House (Princeton): 609-924-1353

Triumph Brewing Pub (Princeton): 609-924-7855

Delaware & Raritan Canal State Park (Somerset):
732-873-3050

Griggstown Canoes (Griggstown): 908-359-5970

Appleton Inn (Tinton Falls): 732-389-2100

Forsgate Country Club (Jamesburg): 732-521-0070

7

Historic Towns of the Delaware River

Getting there: From northern New Jersey take the Garden State Parkway or New Jersey Turnpike to I-78 west to I-287 south to U.S. 202 south to State 179 south into Lambertville. From the Trenton area take State 29 north into Lambertville. From the downtown Philadelphia area take I-95 north, then pick up State 29 north after crossing the Delaware River.

Highlights: Riverside sites, outlet shopping, a covered bridge, a steam train, antiques, and mule barges on the D & R Canal.

The Delaware River is a wide, busy, commercial throughway at its southern end as it courses through the tristate ports of Philadelphia, Camden, and Wilmington, Delaware. But north of Trenton, the river becomes slimmer, curvier, more photogenic, favored by canoeists, inner-tube drifters, and folks who just love gazing out on the ribbon of water separating New Jersey from Pennsylvania—and crossing the occasional bridge to see what their neighbors on the other side are up to.

The New Jersey side of the river abounds with historic towns on and around State 29, a rural road that mostly hugs the river as it winds its way north from the intersection with I-95 past farms, parklands, and country cottages.

Some communities, such as tiny riverside Titusville, are quiet residential zones that seem little changed as the years go by. Others, such as Lambertville, have metamorphosed in the past 20 years into major tourist meccas, with numerous antique and collectible shops, restaurants, and country inns. Still others, such as lovely Frenchtown and Stockton, have found a middle ground, offering fine dining, some collectible shops, and an inn or two, but otherwise holding fast to their basically noncommercial rural nature.

Given over completely to history is Washington Crossing, where in the winter of 1776 George Washington and his 2,400 troops crossed the Delaware into New Jersey bound for the battles of Trenton and Princeton, major turning points in the American Revolution.

This three-day journey takes in all those riverside sites, plus a few significant inland ones, among them: Flemington, best known today as an outlet shopping destination but more significant historically as the site of the 1935 Lindbergh baby kidnapping and murder trial; Rosemont, where you can buy fine reproductions of Early American and Shaker furniture from a factory complex housed in former chicken coops; and the Green Sergeant Bridge, the last of New Jersey's 75 covered bridges.

Although you can complete the trip in a long weekend, you will need a lot more time if you want to seriously peruse Lambertville's numerous antique shops, spend a leisurely time in Flemington (maybe doing some outlet shopping or hopping the steam train to Ringoes and Lambertville), or wile away a few hours on the Delaware—canoeing, tubing, or taking the mule barge from New Hope, Pennsylvania.

It's only fitting that we should start our Delaware River jaunt in Lambertville, for this Victorian town is the center of the region's transformation from an often overlooked poorer cousin of popular Bucks County, Pennsylvania, across the river, to a thriving weekend getaway drawing those seeking antiques, historic architecture, and country inns. The bad news, of course, is that on weekends Lambertville can positively bulge with tourists, with streets clogged and parking hard to find. If you can get away on a Friday or stay for a Monday, our advice is to do your country driving on the weekend and save Lambertville for a weekday, when it effuses a more tranquil, down-home feel.

The town is made for walking, so park your car as soon as you can and explore on foot, armed with a copy of the self-guided Lambertville walking tour (available in many stores).

Meandering down Bridge Street (aptly named, since it leads directly onto the bridge into New Hope, Pennsylvania), you'll see a smorgasbord of architectural styles: Queen Anne, Federal, Georgian, Gothic, and Italianate Victorian among them. Be sure to stop at the James Wilson Marshall House at 60 Bridge Street, which has displays of historical photographs and memorabilia from the community. The Federal-style 1810 mansion, which is headquarters for the Lambertville Historical Society, is open from April through November.

Down the road at 32 Bridge Street, the preserved 1812 Lambertville House was a stagecoach stop that played host to Andrew Johnson, Gen. Ulysses S. Grant, and Gen. Tom Thumb, the famous circus midget, who stayed there with the circus troupe in 1867.

Each December the historical society holds an open house tour, taking in the above sites as well as other historical gems not otherwise accessible to the public. The tour portrays the community's past as a thriving mill town, settled in 1705. Strategically set on the Delaware along the main stagecoach route between New York and Philadelphia,

Lambertville was also able to capitalize on its location along the Delaware and Raritan feeder canal (D & R Canal) to the bustling Trenton–New Brunswick Canal system.

Today the D & R Canal is the centerpiece of Delaware & Raritan Canal State Park, where cyclists and pedestrians can follow a tranquil 50-mile stretch of towpath, mostly along the water. A particularly popular portion of the towpath is the 23-mile stretch between Frenchtown and Washington Crossing State Park, all of which is easily accessible from adjacent State 29.

The old Delaware & Raritan Canal isn't the only old thing that's been put to good use by and for modern folks. Once-decaying Colonial houses in and around Lambertville have been bought and refurbished by young urban couples fleeing the crime and congestion of Philadelphia and Trenton. And restored buildings all along Bridge and Union Streets have been given new life as shops selling paintings, antiques, and crafts.

To get a heaping dose of collectibles, head to The People's Store, a giant edifice at Union and Church Streets. Built in 1859 as a dry goods and furniture store, today it's Lambertville's largest antique center, with artists' studios and some 30 shops selling everything from furniture to toys and books.

Another renovated building is The Porkyard at 8 Coryell Street, beside the canal. Once a sausage factory, it now houses antique stores and the Coryell Art Gallery, where you can find the works of some of the Delaware Valley's best artists and craftspeople.

Nearby, the old Lambertville Railroad Station has also been restored and put to good use. It's now the Lambertville Station restaurant and tavern, and adjoins a pretty antique-filled hotel called the Inn at Lambertville Station.

But the Lambertville train station itself is far from defunct. On Sunday from May through October, you can hop the Black River & Western Railroad scenic train for a

45-minute journey along the river and canal, through the woods to Ringoes, and onward (another 45 minutes) to Flemington.

If you happen upon Lambertville at the end of April, you'll likely run smack-dab into the shad festival, since 1982 an annual institution with a huge shad dinner, shad fishing demonstrations, historical tours, and activities for children. One Ted Lewis, who operates the last commercial shad fishery on the nontidal portion of the Delaware, was the inspiration for the celebration, as he continues a more than 100-year-old tradition his father began in 1888.

New Hope, Pennsylvania, Detour

If you've got a hankering to visit Lambertville's bigger sister, New Hope, Pennsylvania, walk or drive down Bridge Street and cross the bridge and you'll be in the heart of this trendy town's shopping and arts area. New Hope is like Lambertville only more so—more stores, more restaurants, more inns. A night in New Hope could start out with dinner at Mother's Restaurant, 34 N. Main Street, a laid-back place with reasonably priced pastas, fish, and vegetarian dishes, and sinful desserts. Then take in a show at the much-respected Bucks County Playhouse, which has performances in spring, summer, and fall.

For bedding down on the Pennsylvania side of the Delaware, drive seven miles north of New Hope on State 32 to Lumberville, where the historic Black Bass Hotel has rooms with balconies overlooking the river. (Be sure to ask for a riverfront room, and be aware that most rooms share a hall bath.) The Black Bass also has a romantic restaurant overlooking the river. Reservations are strongly recommended.

An especially fun excursion out of New Hope is the one-hour ride along the canal on a mule-drawn barge. The barge, which sometimes has live banjo music, operates from April 1 to November 15, and on an abbreviated schedule (Wednesday, Saturday, and Sunday) at other times. The mule barge landing is on the canal towpath south of Mechanic Street, between State 32 and South Main Street.

On weekends year-round, there are big doings two miles south of Lambertville on State 29, where the gigantic Lambertville Antiques Flea Market attracts thousands of serious collectors as well as mere browsers from dawn until 4:00 P.M. on Saturday and Sunday. This is one of the largest and most popular flea markets on the East Coast, and serious shoppers show up early to snatch the best offerings, be they Depression-era glass, antique doll parts, or old comic books.

About a half mile south of the Lambertville Antiques Flea Market, watch for the signs for the Howell Living History Museum on your left. Turn left onto Valley Road, which will take you to the museum. Howell is a working version of an early 1900s farm. The kids will love all the animals, and in fall, there are hayrides, pumpkins, and a ciderfest. Call ahead for hours, since the farm is not open to the public every day and the schedule changes.

Back on State 29, the drive south is a pleasant one under aged shade trees. On nice days you'll see loads of cyclists, runners, and dog walkers along the towpath between the canal and the river; you may even want to pull over and join them for a while.

About four miles south of Lambertville on State 29, look for a green sign on your right identifying Titusville; follow the sign to the right over the narrow bridge that crosses the canal, and turn left onto the dirt road on the other side. There, tucked between the canal and the river, you'll find yourself in one of the area's prettiest little communities—and one missed entirely by most outsiders. Titusville is less than one and a half miles long, so drive slowly on the narrow road to take it all in. There are simple wooden cottages, some with gazebos and steps leading to the riverbank and private piers, as well as old stone houses dating to the 1830s, with plaques stating their heritage.

This stretch of road is called River Drive—not to be confused with River Road, which is State 29. Keep going south on this little drive and you'll soon come to the area's most important historical site, Washington Crossing State Park, an 800-acre woodland abutting the point where General Washington and his Continental army crossed the Delaware that famous Christmas night in 1776.

A plaque facing the Delaware describes the crossing and the ensuing battles in Trenton and Princeton that became the turning points in the Revolutionary War. On Christmas day each year, there's a reenactment of Washington's crossing, with volunteers outfitted in period dress and firing muskets. You can reenact the crossing any old time; don't forget your three-cornered hat, but leave the firearms at home.

The grove alongside the river is a fine place to picnic, with lots of tables and benches. For a nice bit of leg-stretching, walk up the little hill from the river to the canal and stroll along the towpath.

For a more in-depth study of the park and its history, follow County 546 west across State 29 (eastbound, the road crosses the Delaware into the Pennsylvania-administered portion of Washington Crossing) and follow the signs to the park visitors center, which has displays of Revolutionary War–era artifacts and documents. Not far from the visitors center, the preserved 1740 Ferry House Tavern is believed to be the actual building where Washington worked out his strategy for the attack on Trenton.

Also on the grounds are nature trails, picnic and barbecue sites, and an open-air theater with musical and theatrical performances throughout the summer.

From the Washington Crossing visitors center, continue west on County 546 to the stoplight intersection with County 579. Turn left onto County 579 north (the route number may not be marked, but look for the sign marked "Harbourton"). County 579 winds past planted fields, grazing horses and cows, and small houses with neatly trimmed lawns and picket fences before it dead-ends at State 31. Turn left onto State 31 north.

At the intersection with U.S. 202, you will have to make a decision. If you want to visit Flemington to explore the historic district, hop the Black River & Western Railroad train to Ringoes and Lambertville. To do some outlet shopping (see Flemington Detour) take U.S. 202 north, following the signs marked "Flemington via Main Street," which will take you directly into the historic district and, beyond that, mall land.

Otherwise, cross under U.S. 202 through Ringoes to State 179 and the continuation of County 579 north. Ringoes is a sleepy, little Colonial town, with little to see other than the small museum at the Black River & Western Railroad stop and the Bloomin' Onion, a popular country restaurant housed in an 1811 native sandstone building. If you feel like picking your own veggies in season, stop by the Whistle Stop Nurseries & Farm on John Ringoe Road (County 579) near the railroad station.

Flemington Detour

Enter Flemington via the Main Street exit off U.S. 202, making the jug handle across 202 onto Main Street. In five minutes you'll be in the heart of the historic town. Main Street is a beautiful tree-lined road, a world away from the commercial clutter of the outlet shops. Park your car and start walking. At the corner of Main and Court Streets is the site of the Hunterdon County Courthouse, where in 1935 Bruno Richard Hauptmann was tried and convicted of the kidnapping and murder of the Charles Lindbergh baby. Across the street at 76 Main Street stands the Victorian Italianate Union Hotel (now a restaurant), where reporters from all over the world stayed during the so-called Trial of the Century. Each year in October during Flemington Days the trial is reenacted.

If you turn left onto Court Street, then left onto Park Avenue and right onto Bonnell Street, you'll come to Fleming Castle (5 Bonnell Street), once home to Samuel Fleming, who founded Flemington in 1756. In its early days the house served as an inn and stage depot, and was frequented by Patriot leaders and Hunterdon men who distinguished themselves in the Revolutionary War. Today, the place is a Colonial museum run by the Daughters of the American Revolution.

Take your time walking around this tranquil part of town. Despite Flemington's bad press as a charmless modern shopping zone, some 65 percent of the town's buildings are on the National Register of Historic Places.

If you're in Flemington the week before Labor Day, you'll likely see the annual Flemington Fair, since 1858 an agricultural and livestock festival with lots of food and entertainment. It will give you a taste of the town's pastoral character before the outlet shops proliferated around 1965.

Can't resist shopping? You won't have any trouble finding the outlet shops—they're all around, with signs directing you at every corner.

If you want to take the scenic Black River & Western Railroad to Ringoes and Lambertville, head for the train station at the Liberty Village Outlet Center off State 12. Call ahead to check the schedule. The stretch from Flemington to Ringoes (via steam engine) operates weekends from April through December as well as Thursday and Friday in July and August, plus several holidays. From Ringoes to Lambertville (where a diesel engine takes over) the train runs from June through August, on Saturday nights only. The round-trip journey along the entire route is about two and a half hours.

The train is a great antidote for the bustle of the outlet shops and the weekend crowds at Lambertville. Bring a picnic lunch and have a moving feast as the train toots through the farmlands and woods of central Jersey.

Leaving the train station at Liberty Village Mall, head west on State 12 and around the traffic circle, following the signs to Stockton and County 523 south, a winding road that cuts through some of Hunterdon County's prettiest farmlands.

If you've skipped Flemington and have remained on County 579, continue to the intersection with County 523, and turn left onto County 523 south. This road will take you right into Sergeantsville, an important Patriot plotting spot during the Revolutionary War. It is a fun walking town, with restored Colonial houses, an old-fashioned country store, and several antique shops. The beautiful stone Sergeantsville Inn at the corner of County 523 and County 604 was once a tavern where the Patriots gathered to fan the fires of the revolution and recruit soldiers. These days it repeatedly wins awards as one of the most romantic restaurants in the state, with quality eclectic continental food.

Heading west out of Sergeantsville on County 604 (also called the Rosemont-Ringoes Road), you'll cross the Wicke-cheoke Creek. About a mile southwest of the creek is the Green Sergeant's Covered Bridge, the last of 75 covered bridges that once stood in New Jersey, with wooden floor-boards that clank loudly as you cross. You can cross through the bridge only westbound. Eastbound, you must go around it to the right, then make a U-turn and go through.

A little ways farther on County 604 at the intersection with County 519 you'll come to the diminutive town of Rosemont. It is famous today for Cane Farm Furniture, a factory and showrooms featuring reproductions of Early American, Colonial, and Shaker furniture set in converted chicken coops and run by Phil Cane, a one-time chicken farmer. If you liked the period furniture at the Sergeantsville Inn, you can dupli-cate it here, since Cane was the manufacturer. After browsing through the furniture "coops," be sure to drive farther into the complex, where you'll find the Rosemont Post Office—also housed in a one-time chicken coop. There's precisely one parking space, appropriately marked "Customer."

Across the street from Cane Furniture at County 519 and County 604, the Cafe at Rosemont, which is housed in the town's old general store, is a friendly place to have breakfast (closed Monday) or dinner (Thursday through Sunday). The café features New American cuisine, such as salmon steak with pesto sauce and Brazilian-style chicken.

Before leaving Rosemont, stop at Lots of Time Clock Shop, at a curve of County 519 just south of Cane Farm. The shop is filled with antiques, old glass, and, of course, lots of clocks.

Head out of Rosemont on County 519 north (a left turn out of Cane Farm Furniture) through rolling hills and horse farms. Turn left onto State 12 west, and follow this all the way to the Delaware River community of Frenchtown.

Tiny Frenchtown, an early ferry site, feels a lot like Lambert-ville did before it became popular with tourists. There's a genuine residential feel here, and very little ado. The snazziest place in town is the riverside Frenchtown Inn, considered one of New Jersey's finest restaurants. A more down-home place to eat is the Race Street Cafe, sandwiched between two antique stores at the nonriver end of Bridge Street. Savvy antiquers consider Frenchtown's few collectible and craft shops equal to or better than those in Lambertville. A lovely bed and breakfast in town is the Hunterdon House at 12 Bridge Street, a gingerbread-adorned Victorian building that, except for the absence of the Atlantic Ocean, will make you feel as though you're in Cape May.

Perhaps the most interesting thing about Frenchtown is how it got its name. In 1794 a Swiss national named Paul Henri Mallet-Provost bought a large tract of land near the ferry site and set up housekeeping. The locals assumed him to be French and started calling the place Frenchtown. He had, in fact, sailed from Paris—just one step ahead of the French police, who were after him for helping some of his aristocratic countrymen escape revolutionary mobs.

Leaving Frenchtown via Bridge Street, look carefully for the sign for State 29 to Lambertville. Believe it or not, for such a small town, the sign is easy to miss, so don't hesitate to ask directions from the locals.

About nine miles south on State 29, just north of Stockton, you'll come to Prallsville Mills, a complex of nine 18th-century buildings along the Delaware & Raritan Canal that have been restored and converted into a historical site. On Sunday there are guided tours of the old gristmill, granary, and linseed oil mill. Numerous events are held here year-round, including antique shows, design exhibits, and craft festivals.

The Delaware & Raritan Canal and a woodsy section of the towpath run right behind the mill, making for a lovely walk looking out on the canal and, beyond, the Delaware River—a particularly tranquil experience in late afternoon and around sunset.

Just south of Prallsville Mills is Stockton, another sleepy ferry town that's been content to let more ambitious places such as Lambertville and New Hope steal the tourist thunder. Of course, Stockton's not exactly unknown. Colligan's Stockton Inn, a stone hotel on State 29 dating to 1710, was immortalized by Broadway's Richard Rodgers, who wrote a song about "a small hotel with a wishing well" for the musical *On Your Toes.* The wishing well that captivated Rogers still stands in the back patio of the inn, and visitors toss in pennies for good luck.

Equally enthralling are the murals on the inn's dining room walls. Artists painted the Colonial-era scenes during the Depression in trade for food and drink.

Across from the Stockton Inn, Meil's Restaurant and Bakery is an informal place to have breakfast, preferably on the outdoor terrace; for provisions, try Errico's Market across the street and, just down the block, Phillip's Fine Wines.

Heading south on State 29 from Stockton, the old stone churches and stone-and-wood-frame houses preserve a Colonial and Revolutionary War ambiance that's unique to this part of New Jersey. Looking out on the canal and the towpath, you can visualize the old mule barges—and may even catch sight of the tourist barge from New Hope!

As State 29 crosses under U.S. 202, the road briefly loses its country charm as it suddenly becomes a four-lane highway. But it quickly regains its rural feel as it slims down alongside the farms and tiny residential areas on the outskirts of Lambertville.

Soon you're back at Bridge Street, with the option of turning right into downtown Lambertville, or continuing south or east for just a bit more time enjoying the quiet beauty of the region's untrammeled country roads.

For More Information

All establishments are in New Jersey unless otherwise indicated.

Lambertville Historical Society: 609-397-0770

Delaware & Raritan Canal State Park: 609-397-2949

The People's Store (Lambertville): 609-397-9808

The Porkyard (Lambertville): 609-397-2088

Coryell Art Gallery (Lambertville): 609-397-0804

Lambertville Station: 609-397-8300

Inn at Lambertville Station: 609-397-4400

Black River & Western Railroad (Lambertville): 908-782-9600

Full Moon Restaurant (Lambertville): 609-397-1096

Bridge Street House (Lambertville): 609-397-2503

Mother's Restaurant (New Hope, Pennsylvania): 215-862-9354

Bucks County Playhouse (New Hope, Pennsylvania): 215-862-2842

Black Bass Hotel (Lumberville, Pennsylvania): 215-297-5815

Canal Mule Barge (New Hope, Pennsylvania): 215-862-2842

Howell Living History Museum (Lambertville): 609-737-3299

Washington Crossing State Park (Washington Crossing): 609-737-0623

Whistle Stop Nurseries & Farm (Ringoes): 908-788-8552

Liberty Village Outlet Center (Flemington): 908-782-8550

Flemington Information Center: 908-806-8165

Cabbage Rose Inn (Flemington): 908-788-0247

Jerica Hill Bed and Breakfast (Flemington): 908-782-8234

Sergeantsville Inn: 609-397-3700

Cane Farm Furniture (Rosemont): 609-397-0606

Cafe at Rosemont: 609-397-4097

Frenchtown Inn: 908-996-3300

Race Street Cafe (Frenchtown): 908-996-3179

Hunterdon House Bed and Breakfast (Frenchtown):
   908-996-3632

National Hotel (Frenchtown): 908-996-4871

Prallsville Mills (Stockton): 609-397-2793 or 609-397-3585

Colligan's Stockton Inn: 609-397-1250

Woolverton Inn (Stockton): 609-397-0802 or 888-AN-INN-4U

8

New Jersey's Heartland
Three Pastoral Counties

Getting there: From North Jersey, take I-80 to I-287 south to the Hanover Avenue exit in Morristown. Go east to the entrance of the George G. Frelinghuysen Arboretum on the right. From South Jersey take the Garden State Parkway or the New Jersey Turnpike north to I-287 north, exiting at Hanover Avenue and proceeding to the arboretum.

Highlights: The Frelinghuysen Arboretum, historic Morristown, Black Horse Restaurant and Inn, Hacklebarney State Park, horse country, grand estates, and the Great Swamp.

Morris, Hunterdon, and Somerset Counties make up New Jersey's heartland, where pastoral scenes belie a war-torn past. Horses now romp where generals once marched, and peaceful retreats keep the native fauna and flora safe from the encroachment of suburbia.

Our two-day jaunt takes us from historic Morristown to equally historic Clinton and back again, with museums, wildlife refuges, and some great shopping along the way.

The 125-acre George G. Frelinghuysen Arboretum was originally the summer residence of the Frelinghuysen family. This
was a gentleman's farm, landscaped in 18th-century
pastoral style, with sweeping lawns and natural
woods. Passed on to the Morris County Park
Commission in 1969, the property offers a
wide selection of gardens. You can park by
the Haggerty Education Center and Gift
Shop, with Home Demonstration Gardens
out back and all-American variety winners around
one side. Also close by is the well-done Braille Trail,
with ropes to mark the route and signs in Braille, noting the
texture and fragrance of the flowers, trees, and shrubs along
the way.

The arboretum also has several trails through a wet
meadow, swamp, woodlands, and azalea gardens, and along
the Whippany River to the northwest. The Frelinghuysens'
elegant white Colonial Revival–style mansion is now the
home of the county park commission, striking an idyllic pose
among the trees and stretches of emerald lawn. The arboretum, which also has an art gallery with changing exhibits,
holds a harvest festival every September.

Follow the road through the property to the exit onto
Whippany Road. Turn right at the exit, then left onto Woodruff Avenue. Follow Woodruff for three blocks and you'll come
to the Morris Museum—another Frelinghuysen mansion—on
the right. The museum is one of the best in the state—small
but extremely well done. It offers changing exhibits on everything from quilts to the Etruscans, as well as a permanent collection of fossils, dinosaur tracks, model trains, and more.

Turn right out of the museum and continue on Woodruff
Avenue, which becomes Normandy Parkway; then turn left
onto Madison Avenue (at the Friendly's). Take Madison
Avenue about two miles to Treadwell Avenue, and turn right.
Follow the road to the T, and turn left onto Woodland

Avenue. About a quarter mile ahead you'll see the entrance to St. Hubert's Giralda Animal Shelter/Museum on the left.

St. Hubert's was part of the estate of Geraldine R. Dodge; it is now an animal shelter, education center, and art gallery housing Dodge's animal art collection. The facility has a wonderful gift shop full of all things animal—from sculpture to mugs, T-shirts to jewelry—in nearby Madison.

Head west (turn right) on Woodland Avenue, which will become more and more residential until it ends at South Street. Turn right and follow South Street into the heart of Morristown. Turn left onto Miller Road, then right onto Macculloch Avenue to Macculloch Hall, at number 45. The Federal-style mansion was built in 1810 by George Perot Macculloch, father of the Morris Canal. It has 18th- and 19th-century decorative arts, presidential china, and Oriental rugs, but it is best known for its collection of prints by Thomas Nast, the political cartoonist who created the Democratic donkey, the Republican elephant, and a popular version of Santa Claus. The property also includes a two-acre garden.

Head back to South Street, then continue west to the Morristown Green. Turn right, then left, following the roads around the park. You'll probably want to get out and explore here. The town green is ringed by an odd mix of stores, from a Barnes & Noble to a long-standing pizza place. The green itself is crisscrossed by paved paths, with benches, patches of grass, spreading Kwanzan cherry trees, and a large Douglas fir that is decorated every Christmas. Commanding center stage—along with the pigeons—is a stolid obelisk to the Civil War dead, surrounded by oxidized green bronze cannons.

Two of Morristown's many historic churches face the green. Head toward the Presbyterian Church on the Green, Morristown's first house of worship, erected on the site in 1738; the current building dates from 1893. Behind the church is a beautiful old cemetery, with some 150 Revolutionary War soldiers' graves and gravestones dating from 1731.

When you've finished strolling, head for Morristown National Historic Park, which includes—among other sites—Fort Nonsense, Jockey Hollow, and Wick House. Continue around the green to the stop sign and turn right onto Washington Street. Three blocks down, turn left at the First Baptist Church (1752) onto Western Avenue and up toward Jockey Hollow. In one-tenth of a mile turn left on the small, wooded road leading to Fort Nonsense, so named because, though it was built to protect the area during the war, there was no real action here. The foundations of the fort stand among weeds and grass. A short trail includes signs explaining the history of the fort and what sights you can see from this aerie.

Exit Fort Nonsense and go back down to Western Avenue, following the signs to Jockey Hollow. The road is lovely, passing old houses with large front porches, and draped with trees. About a mile past the U.S. Armory, you'll head right into Jockey Hollow. Follow signs to the Wick House. You'll pass the Trail Center on the right; if you're in the mood to hike, you can park here and take one of the trails deep into the forest (best to get a trail map at the visitors center before starting out, though).

The visitors center is just ahead, with a large parking lot. It has literature and rangers to advise you where to hike and what to see. The center also has a short, grim film on the conditions of Washington's soldiers, who braved the hideous winter of 1779–1780 here. You can also take a two-mile driving loop, which passes by soldiers' huts, the Wick House—which Washington used as his headquarters (you can tour the house)—the trail center, and pull-offs with signs explaining various events. To leave the park, continue past the visitors center and turn right at the stop sign onto Tempe Wick Road.

The road ends, fortuitously, on East Main Street (State 24) in the beautiful little town of Mendham, one of the area's poshest communities. Mendham has just a couple of streets of downtown, with a decorator shop, a few antique stores (Grand Bazaar Antiques is especially nice), and a clock and watch store. Anchoring the town is the Black Horse Restaurant and Inn, which has been in continuous operation for more than 200 years. The restaurant is quite fancy, and extremely popular for Sunday brunch. Reservations are a must. Next door is the less formal pub.

Another four miles down State 24 is Chester. Stay in the left lane and turn left at the light (or go straight ahead and continue to Riamede Farm for apple picking in the fall). You'll still be following State 24, which becomes Main Street in Chester. The pretty white gazebo signals the beginning of town; right about now your credit cards may begin buzzing in your wallet.

Chester is shopper's heaven: packed with antique stores (The Carousel, Aunt Pittypat's Parlour, and Pegasus Antiques among the most treasure filled), antique and reproduction furniture emporiums, and good places to eat. Most of the action is on Main Street, but if you wander the side streets you'll find a wonderful bird store as well as Sally Lunn's Tea Room and Antiques Shop, owned by a British woman and serving true British food, from shepherd's pie to afternoon tea, amid a delightful commotion of antiques.

Hacklebarney State Park Detour

From Chester, continue straight through the light at the end of town. Pass Larison's Turkey Farm restaurant; about a mile ahead turn left onto State Park Road. Follow the paved road for about two miles; you'll pass Trout Brook Farm, offering pick-your-own fruits and vegetables, and Hacklebarney

Farms Cider Mill, where you can stop for apples or cider or a tour (by appointment). The park is ahead on your left.

Hacklebarney State Park lies in a glacial valley, through which the Black River runs. The river is stocked with trout. Hikers can choose from among five miles of trails leading through 200 acres of the park (another 600 acres is for hunting only). Hacklebarney is isolated and wild—a good spot for bird-watching and climbing on the massive boulders strewn throughout. Facilities are limited: a soda machine, picnic tables and grills, and a playground. Bike riding and swimming are not permitted.

To leave Chester, turn left at the light at the end of town, onto U.S. 206 south. If you're there on a Sunday, there will be a flea market on your right, which usually draws big crowds and enough traffic to require a police officer to direct it. Continue on U.S. 206 into Somerset County; in about four miles you'll pass Pottersville Road. The U.S. Equestrian Team Olympic Training Center is off to your right. The center, originally a private estate built in 1916, serves as the business headquarters of the equestrian team and offers a variety of show events, from driving to dressage, during the season— generally from March through October. The biggest event is the Festival of Champions, held every June. The staff at the center will send you a calendar of events if you contact them.

Continue on U.S. 206 through Peapack, where Jackie Onassis had a house. Yes, it's that fancy. This is horse country, and you'll pass lots of pasture rimmed with white wooden fences. When you reach Bedminster, turn left onto Main Street (Route 202), and then turn right onto Route 512 (Liberty Corners Road), right before the railroad tracks. About one and two-tenths miles ahead is the Leonard J. Buck Garden, a rock garden begun in the 1930s to be a natural and peaceful retreat. Wooded trails connect the gardens, which are now owned by the Somerset County Park Commission.

About another mile down the road is the U.S. Golf Association headquarters and Golf House museum, up a wide driveway on your right. The museum contains two floors on the history of the sport and its players; one of the most popular exhibits is a room on Bobby Jones. The museum presents one special six-month exhibit each year, usually highlighting a particular golfer. From the observation deck, visitors can watch the goings-on in the research and test center, where the association does trials on golf balls. Players can also test their skills at one of the various golf video games.

Turn left after visiting the museum and continue back to the main road, then turn left onto County 523. Continue straight through the light and follow the signs to Lamington, past stables and people horseback riding through fields, as wildflowers wave in your wake.

Lamington is historic but small, with just a few buildings. To your right is the charming Lamington General Store, with a big front porch full of birdhouses and an upstairs full of quilts old and new. Across the street is the old white schoolhouse-church.

Continue through town (about half a minute) and turn right onto County 517. About a tenth of a mile ahead on the left is Town Farm Apples, where you might want to pick up a snack (their peaches, in summer, are heavenly). The next town is Oldwick, a much more lively village, with numerous Victorian houses beautifully painted in multiple colors and kept up meticulously.

Continue into the center of Oldwick, which used to be named Old Germantown, because it was settled in the 1740s by German immigrants. There's a pretty white Lutheran church with a very old cemetery, and a picturesque general store from 1760. The Magic Shop, a colorful, bright yellow building full of antiques, is worth a visit. The Tewksbury Inn is a cozy place for dinner.

As you leave town on County 517, you'll see some great views of the hills in the distance. About two and a half miles out of town, you'll find yourself in the midst of forest. At five miles, turn left at the cemetery onto County 512. You'll pass the Fairmount Farm Park, and in three and seven-tenths miles you'll be in Califon.

Turn left at the T onto County 513. Another two and a half miles ahead you'll come to Voorhees State Park, begun in 1929 when Foster M. Voorhees, a former New Jersey governor, donated his 325-acre farm to the state. It has since grown to 640 acres. The office is open until 4:30 P.M. There's a one-mile par-course fitness trail into the woods, along with four hiking trails, the longest of which is a mile. Up the road is Hoppock Grove, with a pond, picnic area, and playground, as well as a trailhead. You can drive a loop around the park. At the end of the loop, turn right and continue south on County 513. About one and a half miles ahead is the turnoff for a scenic view, including Spruce Run State Park in the distance to the west of State 31. A half mile farther, by either car or hiking trail, is the New Jersey Astronomical Association Observatory.

The observatory was built by volunteers in the sixties. It has a 26-inch mirror and a rotating dome. The telescope is big enough to see the bright moons of Uranus and a quasar on the edge of the visible universe. The observatory is open Saturday and Sunday afternoons, with star-watching on Saturday nights.

Turn right out of the observatory, then left, following the signs for County 513 through High Bridge, making a right under the train trestle and a left at the T. Continue to State 31

Old Red Mill, Clinton

and head south. Art's Antiques comes up quickly on the right; the large shop has interesting furniture and, during the summer, lots of lawn ornaments and furniture in the front yard.

At the Hess gas station, bear right on County 513 south. You'll be heading into Clinton, over the small bridge crossing the south branch of the Raritan River. At the first light after the river, turn right onto State 173; go over a cement bridge and make another right onto Main Street, which will take you to the Old Red Mill, the signature of the town. The mill was built in 1812, and has been used for everything from wool and plaster to peach basket production, plus electricity and water pumping. Today the mill houses the Clinton Historical Museum, which is also an art gallery. The 10-acre property has old buildings from the milling days, including a schoolhouse and blacksmith shop, plus a limestone quarry.

You can park at the mill site, visit the museum and village, then cross over the scenic little bridge to the Hunterdon Arts Center on the other side. Then continue walking through the town, where little shops hold forth in colorful, Victorian-style buildings.

Continue out of town by turning right at the end of the museum driveway and getting onto I-78 east. Continue east for about 17 miles. (We apologize for the interstate; the back roads don't interconnect very well in these parts.)

Take exit 33 and head north on County 525 (Martinsville Road, which soon becomes Mount Airy Road). Continue into Bernardsville, with its beautiful homes and the elegant Bernards Inn. At the traffic circle, take the first right onto U.S. 202 north. Exit left onto Hardscrabble Road to the Scherman-Hoffman Wildlife Sanctuary, headquarters for the New Jersey Audubon Society, with 250 acres of hardwood forests, meadows, and streams, as well as exhibits of state birds and wildlife photography. The sanctuary leads guided nature walks, including some during the full moon.

Return south on Hardscrabble Road to U.S. 202 north; then take North Maple Avenue south to Lord Stirling Road (which later becomes White Bridge Road). Turn left toward the Great Swamp National Wildlife Refuge, spanning Basking Ridge and Chatham. The Somerset County Park Commission Environmental Center, which has a large selection of guidebooks and nature books, as well as puppets and educational toys, is on the left. The center is also home to the Minstrel Show coffeehouse on Friday nights. The center is contiguous to the Great Swamp, its neighbor to the east.

The Great Swamp was formed by a glacier, which created a huge lake that has receded, leaving 6,783 acres of precious wetlands. It is teeming with wildlife (and mosquitoes in summer) and is surprisingly untrammeled, perhaps partly because it's a bit out of the way. There are 10 miles of hiking trails.

Farther up the road is another turnoff, where you can hike out to a sheltered wildlife observatory overlooking a pond.

As if all this wilderness wasn't enough, just down the road is the Raptor Trust, a peaceful spot in the forest where birds of prey, as well as some smaller and even domesticated birds, live in large flight cages. The birds here were all injured, sick, or orphaned; those that can be totally rehabilitated are released back into the wild; others get permanent homes, acting as ambassadors for the rest of their breed. The attitude here is that the birds' welfare takes priority. Signs ask that parents keep their children well behaved and quiet.

Continue on the same road, which turns into Meyersville Road, to the end, turn left on Green Village Road, then bear right onto Spring Valley Road, which will take you to U.S. 287 and home.

For More Information

George G. Frelinghuysen Arboretum (Morristown): 973-326-7600

Morris Museum (Morristown): 973-538-0454

St. Hubert's Giralda Animal Shelter/Museum (Morristown): 973-377-5541

Animal Imagery Gift Shop (Madison): 973-377-5541

Macculloch Hall Historical Museum (Morristown): 201-535-2404. Open Sunday and Thursday only, early April through early November.

Morristown National Historic Park: 973-539-2085 or 973-539-2016

Acorn Hall, Morris County Historical Society (Morristown): 973-267-3465. Open Sunday and Thursday only, March through December.

Schuyler-Hamilton House Museum (Morristown): 973-267-4039. Open Sunday and Tuesday only.

Fosterfields Living Historical Farm (Morristown): 973-326-7645. Open Wednesday through Sunday, April through October.

Historic Speedwell (Morristown): 973-540-0211

Black Orchid (Morristown): 973-898-9100

Chand Palace (Morristown): 973-539-7433

Grand Cafe (Morristown): 973-540-9444

Governor Morris Inn (Morristown): 973-539-7300 or 800-221-0241

Headquarters Plaza (Morristown): 973-898-9100

Black Horse Restaurant and Inn (Mendham): 973-543-7300

The Carousel (Chester): 908-879-7141

Aunt Pittypat's Parlour (Chester): 908-879-4253

Pegasus Antiques (Chester): 908-879-4792

Sally Lunn's Tea Room and Antiques Shop (Chester): 908-879-7731

Hacklebarney Farms Cider Mill (Chester): 908-879-6593

Hacklebarney State Park (Long Valley): 908-879-5677

Cooper Mill (Chester): 973-326-7645

Publick House (Chester): 908-879-4800

The Roost (Chester): 908-879-5820

U.S. Equestrian Team Olympic Training Center (Gladstone): 908-234-1251

U.S. Golf Association Golf House Library and Museum (Far Hills): 908-234-2300

Town Farm Apples (Oldwick): 908-439-2318

Tewksbury Inn (Oldwick): 908-439-2641

Melick's Orchards (Califon): 908-832-2905

Voorhees State Park (Glen Gardner): 908-638-6969, 908-638-8500 (observatory)

Spruce Run State Park (Clinton): 908-638-8572

Clinton Historical Museum (Clinton): 908-735-4101

Hunterdon Arts Center (Clinton): 908-735-8415

Clinton House: 908-730-9300

Bernards Inn (Bernardsville): 908-766-0002

Scherman-Hoffman Wildlife Sanctuary (Bernardsville): 908-766-5787

Great Swamp National Wildlife Refuge (Basking Ridge): 973-425-1222

Lord Stirling Environmental Center, Great Swamp National Wildlife Refuge (Basking Ridge): 908-766-2489

Raptor Trust (Millington): 908-647-2353

Great Swamp Outdoor Education Center (Chatham Township): 973-635-6629

Chatfield's Grill and Bar (Gladstone): 908-234-2080

Museum of Early Trades and Crafts (Madison): 973-377-2982

L'Allegria (Madison): 973-377-6808

The Hilton at Short Hills Hotel and Spa: 973-379-0100

Stewart Inn (Stewartsville): 908-479-6060

9

Byways of Interstate 80

Getting there: From eastern New Jersey and New York City, take I-80 west to the Millbrook-Flatbrookville exit, just before the toll bridge into Pennsylvania. At the bottom of the exit ramp, turn left and follow the signs into the Kittatinny Point Visitors Center. From the Philadelphia area, take the Northeast Extension of the Pennsylvania Turnpike to exit 35 (Pocono), then head east on I-80. Cross the Delaware River into New Jersey and take the first exit to the right—National Recreation Area Information.

Highlights: Prime hiking trails, canoeing routes, Moravian stone houses, lush parklands, pick-your-own vegetable farms, and wineries.

Bisecting the entire width of northern New Jersey, I-80 is a prime artery linking the state to its neighbors— New York and Pennsylvania—as well as points west. Although this major highway certainly is no country road, numerous lovely byways and rural communities lie just off it, and the mountain views get quite nice near the Pennsylvania line.

This long-weekend trip starts at the Delaware Water Gap National Recreation Area, where I-80 crosses into Pennsylvania (about 65 miles west of New York). The journey moves slowly eastward, exploring roads and towns north and south of the main highway. We'll explore the prime hiking trails and Delaware River canoeing routes of the Water Gap area, the 18th-century Moravian stone houses of historic Hope Township, and the restored Morris Canal village of Waterloo. Here are lush parklands, pick-your-own vegetable farms, wineries, a wonderful herb farm, and such unusual highlights as a free-range chicken farm, a sentiment-filled pet cemetery, and a fish hatchery that supplies all the trout used to stock New Jersey's 500 bodies of water—from giant reservoirs to tiny streams.

The Kittatinny Point Visitors Center, the main information center for visitors on the New Jersey side of the Delaware Water Gap National Recreation Area and the starting point for our trip, is a good place to get maps of the Water Gap area, including guides for hiking, cycling, and canoeing the Gap parklands. Congress created the preserve in 1965 to protect 70,000 acres of land in New Jersey and Pennsylvania that abuts a 40-mile stretch of the Delaware River nearly to the New York border. From the center's grounds you can also get a spectacular view of the Gap itself, a 1,300-foot-deep channel more than a mile wide cut by the river through the Kittatinny Ridge.

After picking up materials at the visitors center, bear left out of the parking lot. The narrow road you're traveling is the historic Old Mine Road, which is believed to be the first commercial road of any extent in North America. Built in the 17th century, it was used by Dutch settlers to bring copper ore north 140 miles from the Pahaquarry mines, about seven miles north of the Gap, to what is now Kingston, New York.

Today the road is favored for its views of the Delaware River, forested mountains, and waterfalls. Rarely crowded, it's especially popular with bicyclists. If you're so inclined, you might choose to park at one of the day-use parking lots along the road and bike for a stretch. The parking lots are also the starting points of trails, both tough and easy.

Heading north on the Old Mine Road, you'll be a world away from New Jersey's multilane thruways and congested urban centers. All around is lush forest, with breaks affording pretty views of the river and the Pennsylvania side of the Water Gap area. The farther north you go, the more woodsy and lush the scenery becomes.

Twelve miles north from the visitors center you'll find yourself smack-dab in the middle of Millbrook Village, a restored 19th-century farm community. Once a small but thriving town with a prosperous gristmill, Millbrook was outpaced by new technology, and its economy declined in the late 1880s. The final blow was struck when the railroad—which brought prosperity to many towns—bypassed Millbrook, resulting in more of its businesses closing and more craftsmen leaving to find work elsewhere. By the early 1900s the town ceased to exist as a community.

Today old Millbrook has been refurbished, with many period buildings brought from other towns. Each building is furnished with objects that villagers might have used. Early skills and crafts are demonstrated on weekends throughout the summer and during Millbrook Days, a celebration held each October.

Be sure to stop first at the Spangenburg Cabin, where you'll find literature about the community, including a self-guided walking tour. A chalkboard lists daily activities, such as quilting, black-smithing, and shoemaking. There's also a slide show that recounts the history of the area and Millbrook's rise and fall.

Coming out of Millbrook, take County 602 south to Blairstown. This lovely route cuts across the Kittatinny Mountain Range and the Appalachian Trail as the scenery changes from woodlands to rolling farm country, finally depositing you in the heart of rural Blairstown. The town is best known for its private prep school, Blair Academy, and for its airport, where you can take glider rides.

Blairstown is a good place to break for lunch at the Martha Washington Restaurant (the prep school kids like to bring visiting parents here). Lots of lace and doilies give the place an elegant daintiness. The pasta dishes, chicken, and seafood are well prepared and reasonably priced, and the service is friendly.

Leaving the tiny downtown, take Main Street in either direction to State 94; turn left onto State 94 north, then turn right onto County 616 south, also called Cedar Lake Road. The road goes through residential Blairstown, a community of fashionable houses on large landscaped lots. The Cedar Lake Polo and Hunt Club, which will come up soon on your right, is a fun place to watch polo matches on weekends throughout the year (there's an indoor arena for inclement weather) and, if you're so inclined, even take polo lessons. For those who have yet to master a horse, let alone a sport atop one, there are riding lessons for all skill levels, and trail rides that even beginners can handle.

Another one and a half miles down County 616 will bring you to a sight that will tug at the hearts of animal lovers: the Blairstown Pet Cemetery. Here, on an expanse of rolling land amid shade trees, are the graves of dearly departed pets. Many are memorialized in headstones with dedications to Fifi, Pepper, and Rex, among others. Some stones bear a photo of the pooch encased behind protective glass. Others are marked by stone statues of poodles or terriers or German shepherds or, in a few cases, a commemorative red fire hydrant.

Adjacent to the pet cemetery, the Blairstown Nursery and Garden Center is a good place to buy potted plants and fresh flowers; perhaps you'll buy a bloom for one of the doggie graves next door.

Just a few hundred yards back the way you came on County 616 (Cedar Lake Road), turn right onto Edgehill

Road (County 607 south). This winding, hilly road takes you to County 521, where you'll turn right (south). In about one and a half miles look for the signs for Race's Farm Market, one of the area's most popular stops for pick-your-own vegetables and, in fall, fresh cider from the farm's own mill. From County 521, little signs will direct you to the farm market— right onto Union Brick Road, then right onto Hogeland, and right again onto Belcher Road.

The crops change with the season; during an August visit, we had a choice of cabbage, beans, beets, peaches, tomatoes, red raspberries, and all sorts of gourds. We were back in September for apples and fresh cider. The farm market is open from March through December, with the cider season starting in September.

Leaving Race's Farm Market, retrace your drive (left onto Belcher, left onto Hogeland, left onto Union Brick), then turn right onto County 521 south.

Our next stop is Pine Hill Poultry Farm, home of free-range chickens raised without chemicals, hormones, or growth stimulants, and sold (whole or cut to order) out of a 1920s country store. The 32-acre farm is more than just a slaughterhouse, however. Proprietor Gus Belvario will happily take you on a tour of the place, showing how the chickens are raised and introducing you to his two pet goats, Jason and Herman. To get to Pine Hill Poultry Farm, turn right onto Foundry Road a little less than a mile after turning onto County 521 south, then right onto Mount Herman Road, and follow the signs to the farm. Because this is a working farm, visitors are usually welcome only from Friday to Monday, though if you must come at another time, phone ahead and Gus will try to accommodate you.

After visiting the poultry farm, come back on Mount Herman the way you came (turning left onto Foundry Road, then right onto County 521 south). Just a short way down you'll come to a blinking light and find yourself in the heart of the beautiful Moravian village of Hope, one of the state's most charming historic towns. Hope is a walking town, so park your car as soon as possible and explore on foot. The main thoroughfare is High Street, where you'll find 16 preserved stone and brick buildings. These and the cemetery are all that is left of a thriving 18th-century religious community.

The Moravians were a religious sect of German descent who immigrated to this country from Moravia and Bohemia in 1735 to escape persecution. Settling first in Bethlehem, Pennsylvania, a group moved on to Hope in 1769, setting up one of the first planned communities in the country. Sadly, the community failed in 1808 when the mother church in Germany could no longer provide subsidies. The lands were sold, and the Moravians returned to Bethlehem and Nazareth, Pennsylvania, where their descendants still live today.

The last act of the community before abandoning the settlement was a worship service in the community house (called the *gemeinhaus*) on Easter Sunday, 1808. Built in 1781, this Moravian religious center is now the First National Bank of Hope, where patrons can make deposits into an ATM instead of an alms dish.

The Hope Historic District Commission distributes free walking tour maps identifying the town's most important Moravian structures. Guided walking tours of Hope are provided at 10:00 A.M. each Saturday from June through mid-October by a community group called HOPE (Help Our Preservation Effort). The tours, which last about one and a half hours, leave from the Inn at Mill Race Pond, just off the main street on County 519.

The old gristmill on the inn's grounds is one of the most important historic places in town. Built in 1769–1770, this and the millrace were the first structures erected by the Moravians. During the Revolutionary War, grain was ground here for Washington's troops encamped at Jockey Hollow in Morristown.

Today the beautifully preserved buildings that make up the Inn at Mill Race Pond provide a wonderfully atmospheric base for exploring Hope and environs. (We spent the first night of our two-night trip here.) The inn's gourmet restaurant specializes in seasonal menus featuring recipes using ingredients that the settlers were likely to have had on hand.

Heading south out of Hope, pretty County 519 winds past farmlands and cornfields. About four and a half miles south of town you'll come to Matarazzo Farms and the Four Sisters Winery, jointly owned enterprises that make abundant use of the region's agricultural riches. At 400 acres, Matarazzo is one of the area's largest farm markets, where you can pick your own fruits and vegetables in season or buy them ready picked. For a fun break you can go on a tour and tasting at the winery. Both operations are open daily.

Another one and a half miles south down County 519, turn left onto U.S. 46 east. Our next attraction is the Pequest Trout Hatchery in Oxford, which supplies all the brown, rainbow, and brook trout for New Jersey's public freshwater fishing grounds.

But first take time out for some sustenance—a stop at Buttzville's legendary Hot Dog Johnny's, just a mile east on U.S. 46 from the turnoff at County 519. Folks come from miles around to plunk down 90 cents plus tax for the steaming hot wieners with the works (bun, mustard, catsup, pickles, onions) that have been cooked up on this very site since 1935. The stand is now run by the founder's daughter, Pat, who's worked at the place since she was eight years old. Hot Dog Johnny's is also popular for its fresh buttermilk supplied by a local farmer, and birch beer served in frosted mugs.

Now for the hatchery. Continue east on U.S. 46 about three and a half miles until you see signs for the right turn to the state-run Pequest Trout Hatchery and Natural Resource

Education Center, open Friday to Sunday from 10:00 A.M. to 4:00 P.M.

Stop first at the education center, where a 15-minute video explains the workings of the hatchery and describes the trout life cycle. Then head out for a self-guided tour of the hatchery, following the little green trout painted on the pavement. You can see where the trout eggs are collected by a stripping procedure, the tanks where they're hatched, and the huge raceways where they're kept as they grow to harvest size. Some 600,000 trout are taken each year to New Jersey's public fishing waters.

The education center holds classes in fly-fishing and casting for beginners, so you might end up some day hooking one of the very fish you saw growing in the raceways.

Before leaving Pequest, plug a dime into the gum ball machine in the visitors center and get a handful of pellets to feed the trout in the pond just outside the entrance.

Continue east on U.S. 46 for three miles and look for the signs for County 611. Immediately after St. Peter and Paul's Church turn left onto County 611 north—a lovely back route to Jenny Jump State Forest—which passes numerous farms and plant nurseries. About two and a half miles up County 611 follow the signs to Jenny Jump, turning right onto Farview Road and following the woodlands into the 1,300-acre park. Here you can picnic under the trees or take one of several blazed interpretive trails into the forest, from a short .3-mile trail into a marsh to a steep 1.5-mile summit trail that affords gorgeous mountain and river vistas.

After exploring Jenny Jump, retrace your way back to U.S. 46 east (Farview to County 611 south to U.S. 46 east). About one and a half miles down U.S. 46 turn right onto Barker's Mill Road, just after you pass a Texaco station and then a Citgo station. The road winds around and veers sharply to the right about two miles down. Just after you make that

sharp curve to the right, turn right onto Mt. Bethel
Road. A few miles down on your right you'll come
to the Well Sweep Herb Farm (open daily except
Sunday), a cornucopia of some 600 fresh and dried
herbs, the former growing in neat little outdoor bins
and in the protective greenhouse, where flowers
also are harvested. A gift shop houses all manner of flower and herb products, from dried
arrangements to potpourri, seeds, gardening
books, soaps, and even birdhouses. Also on the
property are a variety of fruit trees, a brilliantly
hued flower garden, and a formal herb garden where
all plants are labeled.

A catalog showing all the varieties of herbs and flowers
sold at Well Sweep (the farm does a large mail-order business)
is available free at the property or for $2 by writing the farm
at 317 Mt. Bethel Road, Port Murray, New Jersey 07865. You
can arrange a tour by calling ahead.

Leaving Well Sweep, continue on Mt. Bethel Road in the
direction you were going, and one mile down at the stop
sign make a sharp left onto Rockport Road (also called
County 629). You'll wind past farms and cornfields and really
have a sense of why New Jersey is called the Garden State.
Rockport Road soon merges into Grand Avenue, which takes
you into the center of Hackettstown, a community of gracious Victorian houses and other well-preserved 19th-century
buildings.

At Main Street in Hackettstown, turn right (Main Street
is also U.S. 46 east). At the light, follow the sign to Waterloo
Village, making a sharp left onto Willow Grove Street (also
called County 604). About one and a half miles north you'll
come to the Stephen's Section of Allamuchy Mountain State
Park, a great place to take a break for a picnic or hike one of
the trails, some of which skirt the Musconetcong River, popular with fishermen.

Continuing north on County 604 you'll soon see the Morris Canal and signs to the parking lot for historic Waterloo Village.

In its heyday in the 1830s, the canal was New Jersey's major freight transportation system between Phillipsburg, on the Delaware River, and Newark, moving lucrative cargoes of coal, iron ore, grain, and lumber.

Alongside the canal is Waterloo Village, one of New Jersey's most celebrated restored Colonial towns. It is famous for its summer festival of music and arts, held weekends from May through October, as well as its September antique fair.

Known until 1815 as Andover Forge, Waterloo was a major iron town; in 1760 it had a gristmill, sawmill, and forge, and mansions for the ironmaster and forgeman. The forge itself, which was actually north of the village, supplied cannonballs for the Revolutionary army.

When the Morris Canal opened in 1831, Waterloo's fortunes soared with the canal's. But the coming of the railroad—which initially added to the town's prosperity in the mid-1800s—ultimately precipitated its gradual decline in the early 1900s. This more efficient transportation system eventually put the canal out of business, and the iron industry moved west.

Once a deserted village, the now-restored Waterloo, which is run by a nonprofit arts foundation, offers a fascinating glimpse into 19th-century life in rural New Jersey. The village is open from mid-April to December 31, from Tuesday through Sunday. This is a walking town. Park your car in the lot, pay the entrance fee, and allow several hours to follow the roughly circular route through the village. All of the buildings are original to the village. Some are museums; others house Colonial craft demonstrations. The stately Methodist church has not missed a Sunday service (the public is welcome) since it opened in 1850. The canal museum, which was built in the latter half of the 19th century as a residence for a schoolteacher and later housed a canal boatman, contains a model of the Morris Canal and its system of locks and inclined planes, plus other related relics from the period.

One of Waterloo's newer additions is a re-created 17th-century Leni-Lenape Indian village built on its own island. There's a community longhouse, dugout canoes, tools, and crafts. Along the path through the Indian village, signs explain details of Leni-Lenape life.

A pamphlet with an excellent self-guided walking tour of Waterloo Village is distributed at the gate, and guides in period costumes based inside the buildings give tours of their domain. You can purchase victuals at several spots on the grounds, but instead we recommend picnicking in the shade of graceful old trees along the Musconetcong River, with views of swans and Canada geese.

After touring Waterloo Village, follow Waterloo Road (County 604 east) and at the light turn right onto U.S. 206 south. At the junction with County 183, bear right at the sign for County 183 south (Stanhope/Netcong). When you see the sign for "Historic Village of Stanhope," turn right onto Main Street.

Stanhope is another pretty, small, rural town, worth some leisurely strolling. It's a perfect base if you're planning to visit Waterloo Village, which is within walking distance from town. The town is also just a short walk from Lake Musconetcong, where there's sailing, swimming, and waterskiing. Boat rentals also are available.

Antique seekers not lucky enough to be in Stanhope during Waterloo Village's September antique fair should head four miles north on U.S. 206 to Andover, one of the state's prime antique centers, with shops galore.

Perhaps one of the best reasons to stay in Stanhope is the Whistling Swan Bed and Breakfast Inn, a gorgeous Victorian building in the heart of town at 110 Main Street. Innkeepers Paula Williams and her husband, Joe Mulay, decorated the

inn with antiques handed down by Paula's grandmother. Each
of the 10 guest rooms has its own unique charm, and a private
bath. The couple serve a breakfast of homemade breads, fresh
fruit, and other treats in their formal dining room, and in
good weather you can eat outside on the wide veranda. Paula
and Joe are a gold mine of tips on exploring the area, recom-
mending the best places to eat, buy antiques, and even find
some hot night spots.

After a leisurely visit to Stanhope—and, we hope, a stay
at the inn—it's time to head home. Take County 183 south to
either U.S. 46 or I-80, a short distance away.

You've seen some well-preserved historic towns, walked
some of New Jersey's prettiest wilderness areas, driven a variety of lovely country roads, and maybe picked up some great
vegetables, herbs, and perhaps even a free-range chicken. And
if you haven't, you can always come back along the scenic
byways of I-80.

For More Information

Delaware Water Gap National Recreation Area, Kittatinny
   Visitors Center: 908-496-4458

Kittatinny Canoes: 800-356-2852

Historic Millbrook Village (Millbrook): 609-841-9520

Martha Washington Restaurant (Blairstown): 609-362-6717

Cedar Lake Polo and Hunt Club (Blairstown): 609-362-8227

Race's Farm Market (Blairstown): 609-362-8520

Eagle Ridge Soaring Gliders (Blairstown): 609-362-8311

Pine Hill Poultry Farm (Hope): 609-459-5381

Hope Historic District Walking Tours: 609-459-5381

Inn at Mill Race Pond (Hope): 609-459-4884

Seasons on Mountain Lake (Hope): 609-475-4890

Matarazzo Farms and Four Sisters Winery (Belvidere):
908-475-3671

Hot Dog Johnny's (Buttzville): 609-453-2882

Pequest Trout Hatchery and Natural Resource Education Center
(Oxford): 908-637-4125

Jenny Jump State Forest (Hope): 609-459-4366

Well Sweep Herb Farm (Port Murray): 908-852-5390

Stephen's Section of Allamuchy Mountain State Park
(Hackettstown): 609-852-3790

Waterloo Village (Stanhope): 973-347-0900

Whistling Swan Bed and Breakfast Inn (Stanhope):
973-347-6369

Black Forest Inn (Stanhope): 973-347-3344

The Inn at Old Morris Canal (Stanhope): 973-347-9434

Andover Antiques (Andover): 973-786-6384

Crossed Keys (Andover): 973-786-6661

Mattar's Restaurant (Allamuchy): 609-852-2300

Inn at Panther Valley (Allamuchy): 908-852-6000

Harvest Moon Inn (Ringoes): 908-806-6020

10

Getting High on Sussex

Getting there: From North Jersey or Manhattan, take I-80 to State 15 north (Sparta, Lake Mohawk exit), following the signs into the center of Sparta. From the Philadelphia area, take the New Jersey Turnpike to I-287 north to I-80 west to State 15 north.

Highlights: High Point State Park, Sterling Hill Mine and Museum, a gingerbread castle, a golf mecca, homegrown baseball, and a crafts fair.

Sussex sounds a bit British, and when you're on one of the county's back roads, with sheep dotting green fields and hills rising in the distance, you could almost fancy yourself in the Dales. Sussex County, the northernmost region in the state, is in some ways like an expatriot. No major highways. No factories. But there are castles, and horse farms, and minerals that glow.

Sussex offers the state's heights—High Point State Park—and its depths—Sterling Hill Mine and Museum. It boasts a Gingerbread Castle and the extensive Spa at Great Gorge. Although there are no longer more cows than people in the county, it is still one of the top agricultural areas of the state, with one of the lowest population densities.

The new Skylands Park, home of the N.J. Cardinals baseball team, is fast becoming a summertime favorite. And on
the near horizon is a "golf mecca," with 15 to 20 courses, in
Vernon. Sussex's whirlwind of attractions, natural and man-
made, offer a wonderfully kaleidoscopic agenda for a two-
day escape in the country.

Sparta is a small but busy town, abutting a gorgeous lake. To
explore the lake (which has private houses and clubs all around
it), take State 181 through town to County 613, East Shore
Drive, south. The drive leads you around Lake Mohawk,
where beaches and boating access are available to Sparta residents only. You can, however, walk the old-fashioned boardwalk at the southern end of the lake, in the heart of Sparta.
Here, across the street from the lake, Krough's is a cozy spot
for a meal, particularly in winter when it's toasty warm and
the lake is frozen over.

If you don't care for the boardwalk, when you get to the
T on State 181, turn right. You'll pass Coach House Antiques
and the Sparta Bakery, if you'd like some sustenance for the
adventure ahead. Continue on this pretty two-lane country
road, where you'll get your first taste of Sussex's faded red
barns and undulating green fields. At the light turn left onto
State 15 again, and in another half mile, in season, you'll find
the first of many farm stands selling Jersey corn and tomatoes. All around are fields of goldenrod and wildflowers.

About four miles ahead, near the junction with State 94, you'll
come upon Olde Lafayette Village on the left. A duck pond
brings a bit of nature into the sedate cluster of Colonial-style
gray and red buildings, offering more than two dozen outlet
shops, from Van Heusen to Bugle Boy to Capezio
shoes, along with gift and art shops. The
Lafayette House Restaurant and Lounge
has a pub menu, or you can have dinner in

the cozy dining room upstairs. The Sunday brunch is popular with families.

Turn left out of the parking lot and continue on State 15 for four-tenths of a mile; at the Silver Willow crafts and antique store on the left, turn left and pull into the large parking lot in front of the Lafayette Mill building.

Silver Hollow is just one of many treasure troves of antiques in this tiny outpost. There's a Christmas store in the basement. Next door is the original Lafayette General Store, an unpretentious place with several tables for breakfast and lunch customers (French toast, omelets, homemade soup of the day, sandwiches, and ice cream), plus earthenware, throw blankets, and other country items for sale.

The large Old Armstrong Mill building houses 40 antique dealers and related specialty shops. The main building and several other shops in the complex are closed on Tuesday and Wednesday, but Ivy Antiques is open daily. Stepping inside is total immersion in the old days, complete with big band music on the radio. At the rear of the parking lot are a few picnic tables overlooking the Paulins Kill River.

Return south on State 15 and turn left at the second light onto State 94 north; you may catch sight of some sheep grazing on your right about a half mile ahead. Although cows used to be the major farm animal here, dairy farms are giving way to small sheep farms, as well as horse farms and new garden farms; you'll see "Tree Farm" signs all along the way.

Continue about two miles on this pretty country road and, at the green sign for Lake Grinnell, turn right onto West Mountain Road. You may see some equestrians in training in a field on the left, or some riderless horses simply out enjoying the sunshine. The road is curvy and goes over a narrow bridge; it presents a good picture of the county, with its mix of venerable old houses and barns and spacious modern homes. Still, great expanses of fields remain, fringed by hills to the left and straight ahead.

About five miles along West Mountain Road, turn left at the stop sign onto County 517 north, where you'll be greeted by lovely views of the valley and the hills beyond. In about a mile, you'll come to the Ogdensburg city limits, and quickly see the first sign for the Sterling Hill Mine and Museum.

Skylands Park Detour

Fans of America's great national pastime may want to return to and continue on State 15 north to State 206 in Augusta, and make a right at the light to a real *Field of Dreams*–like setting on your left.

New Jersey has been experiencing something of a base-ball explosion in the last several years, with teams setting up at stadia in Atlantic City, Newark, Montclair, and Trenton. But the highest-profile team is the New Jersey Cardinals, with its Skylands Park stadium nestled among the cornfields and farms. The short-season, Class A club of the New York–Penn League moved to New Jersey five years ago, and plays base-ball with heart.

The stadium offers not only the Class-A club games, but, between innings, contests for kids—weird contests, some-times, such as a bagel race or a dizzy bat race. The park also is home to a museum of baseball photographs and memora-bilia, a sporting goods store, and a complex with batting cages and arcade games. You can even have a picnic on the grounds—with food purchased at the park. They've gotta make back their investment somehow: tickets sell for less than $5 general admission, and less than $10 for reserved seating.

Ogdensburg was built because of the mines. The area claims to have more minerals underground than anywhere else on earth, although it was economical to mine the area only for zinc. Follow the brown, yellow, and white signs to the museum, where you can learn all about the history of the area as well as the mining process in the mine itself, which closed for business about a decade ago.

Brothers Bob and Dick Hauck bought the defunct mine several years ago and are doing a wonderful job of restoring it. A tour includes a 312-foot tunnel with an exhibit of large mining equipment, an ore shoot, and lots of fluorescent minerals. A knowledgeable tour guide—often one of the Haucks—will breathe life into the deserted mine and the fascinating museum, which is filled with old equipment, rock specimens, gold in various forms, and an old safe. The tour can last two hours or more, and includes a 1,000-foot descent into the mine, where you will get some sense of what a miner's life was like. (You'll be startled by how really dark it can be.) The highlight of the tour is the Rainbow Room, where seemingly plebeian rocks turn into burning embers of pink, green, yellow, and orange under ultraviolet light.

The museum has a small food-serving area and a gift shop. The Haucks also have a series of "mining fields," piles of rocks out back to rummage through on your own. The museum is open daily May through October; weekends only December and March.

The rock theme is continued just down the road, at the Franklin Mineral Museum and Mine Replica, opened in 1965. The Franklin ore body was the world's richest zinc reserves and contained 30 minerals found nowhere else in the world; the mine was depleted in 1954.

To get to the Mineral Museum, turn right out of the Sterling Hill parking lot, then make a quick left, going through a little round tunnel (kind of fun). Continue on Cork Hill Road, a rickety two-lane thoroughfare overhung with trees and vines. At the T, turn right onto Franklin Avenue, and make the first left at the blue sign for the Mineral Museum. Follow the signs to the museum.

The re-creation of a mine may be anticlimactic after seeing the real thing at Sterling Hill, but the Mineral Museum has its own strengths. A large room contains more than 300 specimens of rocks from the area; the Fluorescent Room presents a mesmerizing tableau of fluorescing and phosphorescing minerals—your guide will explain the difference.

The museum also has a room of fossils, including a mastodon bone and tusk and a dinosaur footprint. Down a series of stairs in the back of the museum is a tailings pile; for an extra fee, adults can take home up to 25 pounds of rocks and children up to 10 pounds of rocks; you can check whether they fluoresce at an ultraviolet light near the tailings. BYOHOrP (bring your own hammer or pick), although most specimens are small enough to just pick up and carry. The Franklin Mineral Museum is closed from December 1 through March 1.

Next on the itinerary is the Gingerbread Castle. Leaving the Mineral Museum, turn right at the stop sign and left at the next stop sign. Go around the pond and continue to State 23. Turn left and head north; the road begins with quaint farm stands but turns quickly into a long stretch of fast-food places and gas stations. About two and a half miles down the road, you'll come upon the blue, pink, and chrome Memory Lane Cafe, serving hot dogs, burgers, and a heap of nostalgia with its oldies jukebox and yellow Texaco gas pump. Another half mile ahead in the town of Hamburg, just after the overpass, the Gingerbread Castle looms large down Gingerbread Castle Road. The strange pink castle was the brainchild of a successful businessman who hired Joseph Urban, stage designer for the legendary Flo Ziegfeld (of Ziegfeld Follies fame), to carry out his fantasy. The castle is filled with fairy-tale scenes, inside and out; children dressed like Hansel and Gretel serve as guides. The castle fell into disrepair for a while but was reopened a decade ago. The little train ride that old-timers recall from their childhood no longer runs, but now there's a snack bar and gift shop, and you can picnic on the lovely grounds near the Wallkill River. The castle is open only in the summer, and during Halloween, when it becomes haunted.

Return to State 23 and continue north another mile to State 94. This road leads to ski country, Jersey style, in winter. In the spring, summer, and fall, it is full of crops, lush fields, and pretty farmhouses. Germans settled here a century ago because it reminded them of Bavaria, and you can understand why along this road.

About four miles ahead, the pastoral scenery becomes dominated by Vernon Valley/Great Gorge, the biggest ski area in the state, which also claims to have the biggest water park in the world. You'll pass right by Great Gorge Village, which features a $12 million spa with Kites Restaurant above it, and a condo village (you can ski from your front door). Across the road is Seasons Riding Stables. Golfers can choose from among the Spa Golf Course, the Course at Crystal Springs, and the 27 holes at Great Gorge Country Club.

Continue along State 94 and you'll come to an area serving as water park in summer and ski slopes in winter. Action Park has more than 70 water rides, some of them quite terrifying. Great Gorge also hosts a full schedule of ethnic festivals throughout the summer. In winter, skiers can choose from 52 trails and 17 lifts, with a 1,023-foot vertical rise; the lift lines can be long, particularly on weekends.

Another three miles ahead, turn right at the T onto County 515 south; turn left a half mile ahead onto Breakneck Road, and you'll quickly come upon a skier's hidden treasure in Hidden Valley. Although much smaller than Vernon Valley/Great Gorge, Hidden Valley still has terrain for all levels on its 12 trails, and has virtually no lift lines because management limits the number of lift tickets sold each day. There's a cozy lodge, from which parents can keep an eye on their kids. Hidden Valley is also developing a condominium community.

Return to State 94 and head north to County 644; turn left at the Cardinal Art Gallery (specializing in wildlife art) in Vernon. At the T turn left again and continue south on pretty County 517, lined with old barns, stately old homes, and tidy new ones (and lots of hidden driveways, so be careful). The road feeds into State 94 south, past the George Inn (country and western line dancing on Fridays). Turn right at the junction with State 23 north in Hamburg.

When you turn north, you'll see a delightful old Victorian building with a porch full of country crafts and faux sunflowers, or whatever's in season. Turn left into the Merry-Go-Round and get ready for sensory overload: waves of candle and potpourri aromas, knickknacks and doodads, dried flowers, and small bears form a wild kaleidoscope for your eyes. Not a place for the claustrophobic, to be sure. For those into country crafts and calico, there's plenty to see, squeezed even into the closets of this grand former residence. Don't overlook the matching pink barn out back, with two floors of braided rugs and furniture, some of it hand-painted.

About three miles ahead on State 23 is Katterman Farms, a large farm stand, followed by the Dutch-style Holland America Bakery. Another mile ahead is the town of Sussex, whose major claim to fame is the terrific air show held every August.

Follow State 23 through town and you'll continue on pastoral roads for about seven miles, until you notice that you're going up goodly grades, climbing higher and higher to High Point State Park. The road will lead you right into the park. You can stop at the park office for maps, information, and recreation advice. The pay phones on the side of the building are usually in use by backpackers taking a break from their trek along the Appalachian Trail, which cuts through the length of the park. There are campsites here, too. The scenic drive through the park will take you past a beach, the nature center, and the monument. In good weather the monument area gets extremely crowded, since people enjoy the 360-degree view from New Jersey's acme, at 1,803 feet. You can climb to the top of the 220-foot obelisk, a monument to war dead.

Most of the 14,000 acres of the park were donated to the state by Col. and Mrs. Anthony Kuser of Bernardsville. The park includes the Dryden-Kuser Natural Area, a protected area with a cedar swamp and pleasant hiking.

You'll probably see deer at High Point; let them remind you to keep your eyes peeled on all the roads in this area—both to see more of them (and possibly foxes, wild turkeys, or woodchucks), and to keep from running into any of them.

Continue north out of the park on State 23 to the first left, following the arrows to Deckertown Turnpike and Stokes State Forest, on Sawmill Road. You'll be plunged into deep forest. About two and three-tenths miles ahead at Sawmill Lake are campsites to the left, and a bit farther up you can see swampy terrain through the trees. Sawmill Road ends at Deckertown Turnpike; turn right and keep going through the forested park.

Deckertown Turnpike (County 650) curves to the right past Mashipacong Pond; follow the road all the way out to the Delaware Water Gap National Recreation Area in Montague. Turn left on the Old Mine Road (County 521), which runs down the length of the Jersey side of the Gap.

Go straight at the light for the Dingmans Ferry Bridge, proceeding another two miles until you come upon Peter's Valley village.

Peter's Valley is home to resident craftspeople who devote the summer months to teaching. The public can take courses in pottery, woodworking, metalwork, and other crafts, or just stop by to watch. Be sure to browse the Peter's Valley Crafts Store, which features the work of the resident artisans as well as other craftspeople from around the country. Above the store is the Doremus Gallery, which has changing exhibits. The crafts store is open year-round. The annual crafts fair, held the last weekend in July, is the center's main fund-raising event and draws more than 10,000 people to this quiet oasis.

Many people who come to Peter's Valley end their day at the Walpack Inn, just down County 615 south (which meets County 521), an idyllic road with big cornfields and rolling hills and an occasional house. The Walpack Inn has wonderful views of the hills and the deer, mounded loaves of homemade bread, and a legendary, dapper piano player, Jim Woolsey.

If you're in the mood to hike, make Stokes State Forest and Swartswood State Park your next destinations. To get there, take the first left into Walpack Center, a ghost town complete with cemetery, and continue on this road, which becomes Tillman Road, into Tillman Ravine, one of the state's special natural areas. Drive north onto Dimon Street, which turns into Strubble Road, past Lake Ashroe to the Stokes State Forest park headquarters. The 15,000-acre park has more than 75 miles of narrow roads and trails. It's less crowded than High Point, a bit wilder and more peaceful.

On to Swartswood State Park. Leaving the park office, head south on Coursen Road and then east on U.S. 206/County 521. Follow U.S. 206 south to County 626 west, through Washingtonville and Balesville. Turn left onto County 627, then left again onto County 521, West Shore, and around Little Swartswood Lake to County 622; turn left and follow the road into the park. Swartswood has three loop trails for day hikes, plus part of the Sussex Branch Trail, along an abandoned railroad track. You can also rent canoes, rowboats, and sailboats. In the winter, there's cross-country skiing, as well as snowshoeing, iceboating, and ice skating.

The romantic Dove Island Inn, on 500 feet of lakefront, offers meals and lodgings, with stunning water views.

Continue on County 622 through the park; the road will take you all the way to Newton, the bustling Sussex County seat, arranged around a village green. There are lots of old historic buildings, including the Newton Fire Museum on Spring Street. In the Sussex County Historical Society headquarters, in the Hill Memorial Building at Church and Main Streets, are area artifacts, including the skeleton of a mastodon found in the sixties. Newton is also home to the Sussex Horse and Farm Show, held at the fairgrounds each August, celebrating the heritage of the area.

To return to Sparta—the starting point of this jaunt—continue on County 616, which leads onto County 517.

For More Information

Krough's (Sparta): 973-729-8428

The Homestead Restaurant (Sparta): 973-383-4914

William C. McNeice Auditorium (Sparta): 973-579-1071

Olde Lafayette Village: 973-383-8323

Lafayette House Restaurant and Lounge: 973-579-3100

Lafayette Mill Antique Center: 973-383-0065

N.J. Cardinals at Skylands Park (Augusta): 973-579-7500

Sterling Hill Mine and Museum (Ogdensburg): 973-209-7212

Franklin Mineral Museum and Mine Replica: 973-827-3481

Memory Lane Cafe (Hamburg): 973-209-0616

Gingerbread Castle (Hamburg): 973-827-1617

Quarry Restaurant (Hamburg): 973-209-4048

Great Gorge Village (McAfee): 973-827-2222

Kites Restaurant (McAfee): 973-827-6111

Seasons Resort and Conference Center (McAfee):
973-827-6000

Action Park at Great Gorge/Vernon Valley Ski Area:
973-827-2000

Hidden Valley Ski Area (Vernon): 973-764-6161

The Lamp Post Inn (Vernon): 973-875-9134

Merry-Go-Round (Hamburg): 973-827-5578

High Point State Park and Monument (Wantage):
973-875-4800

Stokes State Forest (Branchville): 973-948-3820

Peter's Valley Crafts Store (Layton): 973-948-5200

Walpack Inn (Walpack Center): 973-948-9849. Open Friday
through Sunday.

Swartswood State Park: 973-383-5230

Dove Island Inn (Swartswood Lake): 973-383-3336

Sussex Horse and Farm Show (Newton): 973-579-2215

Sussex County Office of Economic Development (Newton):
973-579-0540.

Flapjacks (Newton): 973-579-7555

Memory's (Newton): 973-579-1131

Wooden Duck Bed & Breakfast (Newton): 973-300-0395

Sussex Airport: 973-875-0783

Apple Valley Inn (Glenwood): 973-764-3735

Crossed Keys (Andover): 973-786-6661

Andover Inn: 973-286-5640

The Hayloft (Hardyston): 973-827-2949

Jorgenson's Restaurant (Stockholm): 973-697-7355.
   Open weekends only.

McKeown's (Branchville): 973-948-9915

The Ship Inn (Milford): 908-995-0188

Sirocco's Restaurant (Oak Ridge): 973-697-8828

The Still (Tranquility): 973-852-2437

Craigmeur Ski Area (Newfoundland): 973-697-4500

11

Relaxing Around Ringwood

Getting there: From Manhattan, cross the George Washington Bridge and continue on State 4 west, which leads into State 208 north. Exit at Russell Avenue in Wyckoff. From the south, take the New Jersey Turnpike to State 3 west to State 17 north to State 4 north to State 208 north to Wyckoff.

Highlights: Beautiful parks, Ramapo Mountain State Forest, Ringwood Manor, Wawayanda State Park, a celery farm, a ghost town, and historic ironworks.

New Jersey knows how to build suburbs and it knows how to build gritty cities and it's pretty adept at shopping malls, too. But New Jersey also knows how to hold on to its open spaces.

Our tour takes us to some of the state's most beautiful parks, in Bergen, Passaic, and Sussex Counties, with history hiding among the greenery. Depending on how much walking you do, you can complete this trip in one to two days.

We start in the thick of Bergen County, near Wyckoff. Follow Russell Avenue from the exit off State 208, making a left at the stop sign and another left at the T onto Wyckoff Avenue. Wyckoff is a pretty and quintessentially upscale Bergen County town. A half mile ahead turn right onto Franklin Avenue, proceed through town, and at the small green sign turn right onto Crescent Street; two-tenths of a mile ahead turn left into the James A. McFaul Environmental Center.

The center is a pretty, natural oasis in the midst of suburbia. It's particularly interesting for children, with numerous terrariums in the main building featuring turtles and snakes, and several please-touch exhibits. One large room has picture windows overlooking a pond, where ducks linger placidly even in winter, when the water may turn to ice. Bird feeders attract an ever-changing, hovering parade of winged visitors.

There is an easy nature trail to walk, although it is sometimes heavily used by joggers. Although the center no longer takes in and rehabilitates wounded wildlife, there are owls and deer to visit in enclosures near the lake. Don't miss the charming little garden up the road.

The next stop is Lorrimer Sanctuary, headquarters of the New Jersey Audubon Society. To get there, continue on the loop road through the McFaul Environmental Center and turn right on Crescent Street, then left onto Franklin. At Ewing Avenue, turn left and continue to the sanctuary. The 15-acre haven includes nature exhibits, a bookstore, and easy trails that are especially appropriate if you've got little ones in tow.

For a pretty drive and perhaps more walks in the woods, continue back to Franklin Avenue and turn left. You'll pass rows of pretty houses, small strip malls, and views of the Ramapo hills beyond. In about five miles turn left onto Ramapo Valley Road; go under the overpass and turn right at the second light onto West Oakland Avenue. You'll pass over the little Ramapo River. At the end of the road bear right onto Skyline Drive, one of the prettiest drives in the state (in the winter, one of the least dependable, much to the chagrin of commuters who find it closed during snowstorms).

You'll now be heading into forest country, and quickly come upon the Ramapo Mountain State Forest on the left,

with a pull-out for parking if you want to hike. The Ramapos
are part of the Highlands, a range of ridges and plateaus
formed some 1.2 billion years ago.

Nearby is Camp Tamarack, a Boy Scout camp. About
four-tenths of a mile beyond you'll cross into Passaic County
and the town of Ringwood, just bursting with parks, lakes,
and hiking trails.

Before heading into the thick of things, you may want to stop
at one of the two small shopping centers you'll pass along the
way, where you can pick up beverages and sandwiches.

When Skyline Drive ends at the Wanaque Reservoir, turn
left and continue on Greenwood Lake Road, then turn right
onto the bridge over the reservoir. Continue on narrow, winding West Brook Road (which follows the West Brook) and
turn left onto Snake Den Road. The road will lead you to
Weis Ecology Center.

Weis is one of the state's lesser-known wilderness areas,
and for that reason alone is worth visiting. It's very user-
friendly, with picnic tables, volleyball courts, a spring-fed
pool, and almost a dozen hiking trails, from quick walks to
all-day treks. In the winter, you can cross-country ski; lessons
are offered.

Weis, founded in 1974, is dedicated to conservation and
earth awareness, and offers programs throughout the year,
from hawk watching to hiking and whale-watching (off-
premises, of course). Extremely popular is its Haunted Trail, a
Halloween event. The parking lot for Weis (there's an entrance
fee in the summer) can also be used to get into Norvin Green
State Forest, part of Ringwood State Park.

Ringwood offers more hiking as well as a manor house
and an art gallery. To get there, return to Greenwood Lake
Road and retrace your steps back past the Skyline Drive intersection. Follow the road around the Wanaque Reservoir; at
the fork, bear right onto Sloatsburg Road, which leads you

Ringwood Manor, Ringwood State Park

into Ringwood State Park. Between Memorial Day and Labor Day you'll have to pay an entrance fee at the kiosk at the park entrance.

This area of Ringwood State Park has lots to explore. The Manor House is the most obvious; the imposing Victorian structure almost begs to be toured, and you can do so spring through fall and during the winter holidays. Some guides will tell you about the ghosts. Ringwood Manor, completed in 1879, was the country home of Abram S. Hewitt, the iron-master for the large mining operation in the area. Ringwood was home to many ironmasters before and after the Revo-lution. It's Victoriana to the hilt. It also features a small art gallery; the Ringwood Manor Association of the Arts presents art shows here and in the large Barn Gallery across the pond.

The pond is Sally's Pond, and some say you can see a ghost rising from it. More often, though, you'll see geese. They're everywhere, to the delight of children and to the chagrin of walkers. Anyway, the pond makes for a nice backdrop when you picnic on the sprawling hillside beyond the Manor House. Ringwood also has hiking trails through forests and meadows.

Backtracking two-tenths of a mile down Sloatsburg Road, you'll see the sign for the New Jersey State Botanical Garden at Skylands, on the left side of Morris Avenue. Skylands is the official garden of the state, and though the state can't afford to turn it into a showplace, it is beautiful in its wildness. The Skylands Association helps tend the grounds.

The original manor was established by Francis Lynde Stetson, a millionaire and trustee of the New York Botanical Garden. He hired Samuel Parsons Jr., protégé of Frederick Law Olmsted (who designed Manhattan's Central Park), to lay out the estate. Another garden trustee later bought it and began establishing the gardens that are the basis of what you see today.

There are formal gardens, a bog garden, an azalea garden, annuals, lilacs, wildflowers, and lots more. In the center of it all is Crabapple Vista, a sweeping half mile of lawn and small trees that produce a flurry of white blooms in May. The manor house is absolutely beautiful but nearly empty inside, and open to the public only on rare occasions. Skylands offers walks through the gardens and hikes through the forest, as well as plant sales.

To the northeast of the gardens, on Lake Road, is Shepherd Lake, busy in the summer with swimmers, boaters, and picnickers. Canoes, rowboats, and small sailboats are for rent.

On the second Saturday of the month, you can hear about the ghost town of Long Pond Ironworks. Return to Sloatsburg

Road, turn left, then right onto Margaret King Road. After two and a half miles, turn right on County 511 and continue past the relatively new Monksville Reservoir.

Just past the reservoir, in West Milford, you'll see an ancient-looking church on the left and a nondescript tan and brown wooden building on the right. If you pull in on the right, you can learn all about the ghost town hiding in 55 acres behind this building, which used to be a general store. The Friends of Long Pond Ironworks offer three two-hour hikes through forest and by a waterfall to discover the remnants of an old ironworks, including the foundations of a general store, still-standing workers' houses, furnaces, and a 25-foot pit waiting for an enormous waterwheel that never came. The ironworks was started by British investors in 1766, but during the Revolutionary War the ironmaster made arms for the Continental troops. The tours are a fascinating walk back in time, and the people who run them make them extra vivid because they're so enthusiastic about their history.

If you're in the mood for more hiking, head for Wawayanda State Park, one of our favorite places for such pursuits. To get there, continue on County 511, now called Greenwood Lake Turnpike, to Greenwood Lake. The area here is filled with boat marinas and fishing-related enterprises. Much of the waterfront is privately owned and inaccessible to the daytripper, so continue on, following signs to Upper Greenwood Lake, passing through part of Abram S. Hewitt State Forest. The road turns into Warwick Turnpike; follow it as it curves north around the lake; two and three-tenths miles north is the entrance to Wawayanda State Park.

Although the area around the lake (Wawayanda is from the Leni-Lenape Indian word meaning "water on the lake") is crowded in summer, you quickly leave the picnicking and barbecuing masses behind when you take to the trails—54 miles of them, including nearly 20 along the Appalachian Trail. The park is known for its rhododendrons, which usually bloom in June and July. Boats of all sorts are available for rent on the lake, and there's a beach for swimming and sunbathing. In winter, you can cross-country ski.

Would you believe that a celery farm is the next stop? But along the way are pretty roads and a few other interesting highlights. Here goes. Take Warwick Turnpike back south. When Warwick veers left, continue straight onto Clinton Road. After about five miles you'll cross over the small Clinton Brook and curve over the bridge along the narrow two-lane road. In another three-tenths of a mile you'll catch some sweeping views of the Clinton Reservoir. In another three and a half miles you'll intersect State 23 at the Village Square Inn in West Milford, a former two-room schoolhouse built in the 1880s and turned into a family dining establishment with an Italian touch.

Turn left at the light onto State 23 south, a useful albeit unbeautiful road that follows the Pequannock River, though you wouldn't know it. State 23 swings right into the heart of Wayne, full of basic suburban shopping. At the first light make the U-turn onto State 23 north; stay in the service lane and follow the signs to U.S. 202 north, the lovely Ramapo Valley Road. You'll see houses hidden in the trees, and the Carmel religious retreat on your right, with imposing stone walls. Three miles ahead is the Campgaw Mountain Reservation, which has a small ski area just right for neophytes. Across the road is an Audubon bird sanctuary. Just a few minutes farther north is the Ramapo Valley County Reservation, originally an Indian reservation, then a farm, then site of gristmills and sawmills, and later a bronze foundry. There are a lake, picnic tables, hiking, a swamp, buildings, and ruins. The park is popular with joggers, families, and singles groups.

Just three-tenths of a mile ahead on U.S. 202, turn right onto Darlington Avenue, then turn right again two-tenths of a mile farther onto Campgaw Road, which takes you between the Darlington County Golf Course and the Campgaw County Park. You'll see lots of pretty houses nestled amid the trees. Shortly after the Pegasus Equestrian Center, you'll come to a stop sign. Turn left onto Pulis Avenue, which becomes Forest Avenue; at the fork, bear right onto Hillside Avenue. Watch for a large pink house about two-tenths of a mile ahead. When the road ends, turn left on West Crescent Avenue. Follow it a few short blocks to Myrtle, which feeds into Allendale Avenue, and quickly intersects with Franklin. Turn left on Franklin, and after the first cross street, count three houses on the right. After the third is a small parking area and a sign indicating a state-funded, so-called Green Acres site. Park here for the Allendale Celery Farm, one of Bergen County's hidden treasures.

A celery farm did exist, starting in 1895, but after getting into the wrong hands it fell into disrepair and was eventually turned into a Green Acres site. The Fyke Nature Center oversees the farm's upkeep, with each member getting his or her portion of the 87 acres of wetlands to groom. The main Fitzpatrick Nature Trail goes around Appert Lake, which is home to all kinds of frogs, fish, egrets, kingfishers, swallows, and even an occasional osprey. The area is a favorite of bird-watchers; three observation chairs and platforms have been built, and the quiet birder may spend hours with binoculars in hand.

It takes 45 minutes to walk around the lake at a leisurely pace; along the way, you may see everything from less-than-timid rabbits to orioles or even foxes. Whenever we've visited, it's seemed as though we were the only humans in the place—despite the other cars in the parking area.

The celery farm is one of our favorite places for a quick

retreat from civilization. We hope you love it as much as we do—and don't tell anyone else about it!

From the celery farm, turn left out of the lot onto Franklin Turnpike and left again onto East Allendale Avenue, which will take you to State 17 north or south, and home.

For More Information

James A. McFaul Environmental Center (Wyckoff):
201-891-5571

Lorrimer Sanctuary, New Jersey Audubon Society
(Franklin Lakes): 201-891-2185

Weis Ecology Center (Ringwood): 973-835-2160

Ringwood State Park: 973-962-7031 or 973-962-7047

New Jersey Botanical Garden at Skylands (Ringwood):
973-962-7527

Long Pond Ironworks (West Milford): 973-839-0128

Wawayanda State Park (Upper Greenwood Lake):
973-853-4462

Village Square Inn (West Milford): 973-697-7770

Campgaw Mountain Reservation (Mahwah): 201-262-2627,
201-327-7804, 201-327-7800 (ski area, in season)

Ramapo County Reservation (Mahwah): 201-646-2680

Mason Jar (Mahwah): 201-529-2302

Sheraton Crossroads Hotel & Towers (Mahwah): 201-529-1660

Stacey's Country Inn (Warwick, New York): 914-361-3629

The Woodcliff Lake Hilton (Woodcliff Lake): 973-391-3600

Berta's Chateau (Wanaque): 973-835-0992

Looking Glass Inn (Wyckoff): 201-445-3222

Wyckoff Inn (Wyckoff): 201-891-1929

The Hermitage Victorian House (Ho-Ho-Kus): 201-445-8311

Wooden Duck Country Inn (Greenwood Lake, New York):
914-477-2992

Craigmeur Ski Area (Newfoundland): 973-697-4500

12

Rolling Along the Hudson River

Getting there: From State 4, U.S. 46, I-80, or I-95, take the last exit before the George Washington Bridge, for Fort Lee and Palisades Interstate Parkway. Stay on the Bridge Plaza South to the T, turn right onto Hudson Terrace, and head for Fort Lee Historic Park, on the left.

Highlights: Spectacular views, Englewood Boat Basin, fabulous food stalls, the birthplace of baseball, Yaohan Plaza Japanese supermarket, Beaux Arts train station, Liberty Science Center, Statue of Liberty, and Manhattan sightseeing cruises.

The Hudson River has captured imaginations for as long as there have been people watching it wend its way to the sea from Lake Tear-in-the-Clouds in the Adirondacks. From the Indians to explorer Henry Hudson to the Hudson River painters to Washington Irving and John Burroughs, the Hudson has been a source of inspiration.

We'll use the mighty Hudson and the stentorian Palisades rising from it as the focal point of our trip along the North

Shore of New Jersey, for spectacular views, greenery, and a smattering of history, too.

Fort Lee Historic Park is part of the Palisades Interstate Park system, which includes 2,451 acres in New Jersey and runs along the Palisades, protecting them from development and offering miles of hiking, picnicking, marinas, and lovely views of the Hudson.

You can leave your car in the parking lot and tour the visitors center, which explains the history of the area during the Revolution. If the weather is nice, you might just want to stroll the paved pathways along the Palisades; signs along the way explain the encampment and fort. You can also see a reconstructed battery and soldier's hut. In good weather the park is crowded, with folks walking and taking in the tremendous view to the east of the George Washington Bridge.

On weekends the park also offers music recitals and, during February, a film festival. Fort Lee was known as the Hollywood of the East in the early 1900s. The so-called cliffhanger tale was born here—on the cliffs. Tom Mix strode through, and Mary Pickford made her first movie, *The Lonely Villa,* in the then-dusty little town.

Today, though, Fort Lee is a brash bedroom community for Manhattan, with high-rise buildings and lots of trendy stores and restaurants.

To see the views from the Palisades Parkway, turn right when you leave the park, turn left onto Bridge Plaza, and turn right onto the overpass spanning the entrance to the George Washington Bridge.

You'll drive along Hudson Terrace, past Prentice-Hall publishers and other modern low-rise office buildings, into the very fashionable town of Englewood Cliffs. Down Palisade Avenue to the east are rows of exquisite houses and the prestigious Dwight-Englewood School.

Continue on Hudson Terrace for two miles, then take the entrance to the Palisades Interstate Parkway north.

Englewood Boat Basin Detour

Instead of getting immediately onto the Palisades Interstate Parkway, continue straight at the approach and follow the road down to the Englewood Boat Basin. There's a parking fee in the summer for access to picnic tables, a marina, and stunning views of the bridge and northern Manhattan on the other side of the river. Here, too, you can pick up the Shore Trail, which runs along the river to the New York State border, or the Long Path, at the top of the cliffs.

Continue along the parkway (PIP, as it's affectionately known), and you'll find plenty of opportunities for views. The parkway itself is lovely, one of the prettiest in the state. The foliage pressing right up to the roadway is particularly picturesque in the fall. Watch out for woodchucks, often espied sitting fat and rocklike in the grass.

About a mile north is the Rockefeller Lookout, the first of three official pull-offs for a vantage of the river, northern Manhattan, and the Cloisters—the Metropolitan Museum's branch for medieval art. Three miles farther ahead is the Alpine Lookout and, below, the Alpine Boat Basin. The Blackledge-Kearney House, a Continental army stronghold during the Revolution, is at the base of the Palisades at the boat basin. The house is open weekends for tours.

The nicest place to stretch your legs, though, is about 10 miles farther, at the State Line Lookout. Parking here is free and ample. At the end of the lot is a charming little cafeteria, which takes on extra appeal in the winter when the large stone fireplace is stoked up, providing a warm respite after a quiet hike through the snow. Up here you can connect with the Long Trail, which follows the Palisades up into the Catskills.

On a sheltered bulletin board outside the restaurant is information about activities sponsored by the Palisades Interstate Park Commission, as well as a history of the park. The Palisades, which span 40 miles on the west side of the Hudson, were heavily quarried in the 19th century for bluestone for the streets of Manhattan. In 1900, the commission was established to protect the area, and philanthropists, including the Rockefellers, the Harrimans, and the Morgans, gave money to buy up and protect 14 miles of property, which have remained relatively free of development ever since.

The area also has picnic tables; claim one and listen to the birds sing while you eat.

Continue north on the Palisades Interstate Parkway to exit 4, which will take you around a ramp onto U.S. 9W.

Palisades Cliffs Detour

After getting onto the exit 4 ramp toward U.S. 9W, turn left at the light (instead of veering right to U.S. 9W). Park your car at the turnoff by the New York State border sign. Right over the border is the Lamont-Dougherty Geological Observatory, an important site for seismological data; it's open to the public only on rare occasions, however.

To your right after you park is a wide path leading into the forest. The path branches out in several directions, but keep heading toward the cliffs for the best views. The path also leads to a waterfall; be careful hiking here—the rocky cliffs are tricky. The area is lovely and quiet, and has a stream and lots of birds. Some of the regulars to the site have nicknamed it Paradise. Be warned, however, that if the weather is too dry and the chance of fire too great, the trails will be closed by park officials (check on the bulletin board at the State Line Lookout).

Follow the signs to U.S. 9W south. In a less than two miles you'll pass a sign for the Boy Scout Camp, and a few hundred yards farther, near the entrance to the PIP, you'll see a small bridge going over the parkway and, usually, some cars already parked on the east side of U.S. 9W. If you feel like taking a short hike, make a U-turn, park near the other cars, and walk over the bridge and through the forest to some spectacular aeries at the cliffs' edge. A recently erected fence here may make you feel a little safer. Also nearby is a monument to women's suffrage.

Continue south on U.S. 9W, back toward civilization, past some of New Jersey's most affluent suburban communities. In about two and a half miles you'll see a sign for Closter Dock Road, which leads into Alpine and enviable real estate.

U.S. 9W has some streetlights and a bicycle path. Shortly after Montammy Country Club you'll see a bench on the right; if you were to turn left, you'd head under the overpass to Greenbrook Sanctuary, a pristine nature preserve for members only. Members have a key that opens the gate at the entrance.

In a little less than a mile you'll pass the Clinton Avenue exit, and the scenery changes to office buildings for Lever Brothers, Lipton, and CPC International. At Leo's Restaurant, turn left onto Palisade Avenue and make your first right back onto Hudson Terrace. You'll travel by Fort Lee Historic Park. At the stop sign, continue on Hudson Terrace, although you'll be bearing left. About three-tenths of a mile past the park you'll see a sign for Edgewater and, usually, a man selling hot dogs and other snacks from his little truck. You can park here and hike down to the river and the Shore Trail, or continue your drive down into Edgewater.

Edgewater is a strange jumble of buildings. It's valuable property, being at water's edge and commanding tremendous
views of Manhattan. But vestiges of warehouses and piers
also imbue it with a run-down, waiting-for-revival appearance. It is being revived. Alongside dusty, empty storefronts
are shiny new delicatessens and traditional Italian restaurants.

Continue about two miles and you'll pass the old Alcoa
plant, some say destined to be fabulous condos—someday.
Across the street by the river is a shopping center and an old
paddle wheeler that has been turned into a restaurant,
Binghamton's.

Save your appetite, though; another two-tenths of a mile
up the road, just in front of the traffic jam, is Yaohan Plaza.
Yaohan, a mecca for Japanese expatriots on both sides of
the Hudson, is an enormous food market as well as a strip
of stores selling everything from electronics to the latest robot
toys and golf apparel. The main language of the books in
the bookstore is Japanese. The centerpiece of this wildly
successful complex is the supermarket. The produce section
is quite unbelievable, featuring all kinds of exotic fruits
and vegetables—a visual delight. The aisles are filled with
Japanese cookies packaged with round-faced, smiling cartoon
characters. The selection of fresh fish is extensive, the
variety of packaged and fresh noodles nearly
overwhelming.

All this food will make you hungry, and
wouldn't you know, half the store is given over
to food you can eat on the spot. Food stalls sell
everything from sushi to steamed bean paste rolls, salads, and
noodles. Bring your purchases to the seating area in the back,
where picture windows overlook the Hudson.

When you can tear yourself away from Yaohan Plaza, turn
left and continue along the River Road. You'll pass the
Edgewater Driving Range and Miniature Golf Course, part

of the empire of Arthur Imperatore, a mythic figure of sorts in these parts, who made his fortune in the trucking industry. About one and a half miles ahead you'll see the three round Galaxy apartment towers looming in the distance. The River View Diner on the left is a good place for a quick cup of coffee. Just behind the diner is the Parrot Network, a small store with all sorts of exotic birds. A bit farther down on the right are Country Roads, selling no-nonsense but stylish clothes from Australia, and the Last Resort, with practical and well-made men's clothes, especially sweaters and jackets. Both outlet stores are open on Sunday. About a half mile farther, on the left, is one of the entrances to the Port Imperial Ferry—another jewel in Imperatore's crown.

The ferry service takes passengers to and from mid-Manhattan and lower Manhattan in 10 minutes. Port Imperial also has 90-minute sight-seeing tours of New York Harbor and all-day rides up the Hudson to Tarrytown, New York. There, you can visit the historic Philipsburg Manor working farm, Sunnyside, home of Washington Irving, and the more-recently opened Kykuit, the old Rockefeller estate, with a fabulous art collection and gardens.

There's another entrance to Port Imperial two-tenths of a mile ahead, next to Arthur's Landing (Arthur as in Arthur Imperatore), a lovely place for dinner or Sunday brunch.

You'll be following the road uphill, and in a half mile you'll come to a traffic light. Turn left onto Boulevard East. The Boulevard, as it's known, is an interesting mix of grand old houses and expensive new apartment buildings. The well-to-do Boulevard clashes mightily with the neighborhoods farther inland. Everybody escapes to the promenade and the green parks that follow the river.

About a mile up the Boulevard, bear left onto Hamilton Avenue. Park on this one-block street and walk out onto the small, fenced promenade. A boulder and monument mark the spot where Aaron Burr and Alexander Hamilton held their duel on July 11, 1804. Supposedly Hamilton rested his head upon the rock after he was mortally wounded by Burr.

Follow the one-way roads around the houses back to Boulevard East and turn left; follow the road down past the Lincoln Tunnel viaduct. Stay in the left lane and follow the sign "Thru traffic to Hoboken."

Travel over a bridge and past the Ramada Suite Hotel and a variety of old warehouses, and turn left onto 14th Street. Go three blocks, and turn right onto Washington Avenue, the main street of Hoboken.

The historic town of Hoboken, with its rows of well-maintained brownstones, has been a magnet for urban types who couldn't handle the traffic or high rents of Manhattan. Guess what? Now Hoboken has the traffic and high rents of Manhattan. The cars are parked two and three deep here, especially on weekend nights, when the kids are going to Maxwell's, Boo-Boo's, Texas & Arizona, the Brass Rail, Good 'n Plenty, and other nightspots. The festive nature of the town is in keeping with tradition, since Hoboken was the site of the first American brewery in the 1600s and was rife with Oktoberfests when the German immigrants settled here in the 1800s.

As you drive along Washington Street, you'll understand why people gravitate to the town. Stolid and elegant brownstones strike old-fashioned poses, and the endless rows of shops sell everything from neon clocks to flimsy lingerie. Old corner delis butt up against fluorescent Chinese takeout places and trendy cafés. In the summer, sidewalk cafés blossom; in winter, the kids hang out in the pizza places, looking out the steamy windows at the yuppies hunkered down in their big overcoats.

Hoboken is the birthplace not only of the late Frank Sinatra, but of baseball. At 11th Street, on the median on the right, is a plaque commemorating baseball's birth. Across from the plaque, on the southeast corner of the street, is another institution: Maxwell's. Though Hoboken is now crawling with music clubs, Maxwell's was one of the first, and continues to bring top new bands across the Hudson. The music room, behind the restaurant, is rather dirty and stuffy, but hey, what's a little sweat and germs among rockers?

Also on the east side of the street is the Elks Club, with an enormous elk over the awning, and the Elysian Cafe, reminiscent of the fields that once stretched out where the city now stands. Scenes from *On the Waterfront,* starring Marlon Brando, were filmed here, as well as at other sites in town.

Toward the end of Washington Street, the atmosphere is less charming, with McDonald's, Carvel, and other chain names cropping up alongside squat, charmless buildings— save for the Hoboken City Hall, housing the historical society, at First Street. At the end of Washington Street you'll see the train yards and the superb Beaux Arts train station, a National Historic Site. The station was built in 1907 and has been recently restored. The copper of the building has oxidized green with age; within, the station features a terrazzo floor and Tiffany glass ceiling.

Turn left past the train yards, then make another left; turn right onto Hudson Place and left onto River Street, and one more left onto Newark Street. Here, a large neon finger points down to the famous Clam Broth House, visited by everyone from old-time luminaries to present-day celebrities.

Turn left again onto Washington Street, then turn right at the end of the street onto Observer Highway. This is the gritty part of town, with rutted roads and ramshackle garages. Make your first left onto Luis Muñoz Marín Boulevard. Go under the train trestle; you're now in Jersey City. At your first light, turn left onto 18th Street.

Washington Boulevard skirts the Newport Centre mall complex and apartment buildings, and affords some good views of the river and marina. Follow Washington Boulevard to Montgomery Street, a large intersection that immediately thrusts you into an imposing business center. Turn left onto Exchange Place.

As you round the bend you'll see a striking figure of a soldier impaled by a bayonet. The Katyn Memorial, commemorating the Nazis' murder of 15,000 Polish officers, intellectual leaders, and POWs in the spring of 1940, cuts an unforgettable pose against the Manhattan skyline across the river.

The architecture of the plaza is an exuberant mix of the old and new, with a bow to the old; our favorite building is 101 Exchange Place—steel and glass and very art deco. At the end of the plaza is a pier with benches and plants; in fine weather you'll find people in-line skating, strolling with infants, and relaxing in the sun to the sounds of salsa music wafting out of boom boxes.

Head south on Hudson Street, the first block up from the river; Colgate-Palmolive used to have a plant here, and the enormous dock still stands harborside. Turn right on Grand Street and you'll be heading through the Paulus Hook neighborhood, one of the nicer areas in Jersey City.

Continue on Grand Street to a fork and bear left onto Pacific Avenue, then three-tenths of a mile ahead turn left onto Johnston Avenue. It may look like a vast wasteland, but in less than a half mile the silver dome of the Liberty Science Center will loom on the horizon to your right.

The $65 million center opened in 1992, and features a variety of changing science-related exhibits along with permanent displays of everything from bugs to high-tech computers. Docents offer science demonstrations throughout the day, and there are continuous showings in the center's IMAX theater. Plan to spend several hours at this hands-on museum, particularly fun for inquisitive kids.

The center is part of Liberty State Park, which is still in the throes of development. It is the most visited urban state park in the nation. Continuing right from the center, you'll come upon the parking lot for the Statue of Liberty and Ellis Island Ferry. Farther along, at the tip of the park, is the old Central Railroad of New Jersey Terminal, which is half restored and is the site of annual Rail Expos as well as a variety of concerts. The soaring edifice, with train tracks still leading up to the platforms, almost echoes with the sounds of the eight million immigrants on their way to new lives across the New World. From a plaza beyond the station are fine views of the Hudson.

Continue back up the road and turn left down Freedom Way; you'll catch some good views of the Statue of Liberty. Also along the road is a nature center and nature trail. At the end of the road is a very congested park, a little too busy on a summer day to be much fun. But you can pick up tourist information at the large visitors center, take a peek at the Liberation Monument, and then head back along the nature trail, find a quiet place, and sit down to contemplate the mighty Hudson beyond.

From here you can follow the signs to the New Jersey Turnpike, which will lead you north or south toward home.

For More Information

Fort Lee Historic Park: 201-461-1776

Holiday Inn–Fort Lee: 201-461-3100

Palisades Interstate Park Commission (Alpine): 201-768-1360

Binghamton's (Edgewater): 201-941-2300

Yaohan Plaza (Edgewater): 201-941-9113

Port Imperial Sightseeing Cruises and Ferrybus (Weehawken):
201-867-0777

Spirit of New Jersey Harbor Cruises (Weehawken):
201-867-5518

Arthur's Landing at Port Imperial (Weehawken):
201-867-0777

Shanghai Red's (Weehawken): 201-348-6628

Clam Broth House (Hoboken): 201-659-2448

Ali Baba (Hoboken): 201-653-5319

Liberty Science Center (Jersey City): 201-200-1000

Liberty State Park (Jersey City): 201-915-3400

Circle Line Statue of Liberty and Ellis Island Ferry (Jersey City):
201-435-9499 or 212-269-5755

Circle Line Sightseeing Cruises around Manhattan (Jersey City):
212-563-3200

African American Museum (Jersey City): 201-547-5262

Doyle and Rafferty's (Jersey City): 201-915-9600

Pronto Cena Ristorante (Jersey City): 201-435-0004

Ellis Island Immigration Museum: 212-363-3200

Statue of Liberty: 212-363-3200

The Clinton Inn (Tenafly): 201-871-3200

The Lighthouse Restaurant (West New York): 201-854-1004

American Stage Company, Becton Theater (Teaneck):
201-692-1997

Marriott Glenpointe Hotel (Teaneck): 201-836-0600

Hackensack Meadowlands Environment Center (Lyndhurst): 201-460-8300

John Harms Center for the Arts (Englewood): 201-567-5797

Paper Mill Playhouse (Millburn): 973-376-4343

William Carlos Williams Center for the Arts (Rutherford): 201-939-2323

Index